AUDIT OF THE DRUG ENFORCEMENT ADMINISTRATION'S CONFIDENTIAL SOURCE POLICIES AND OVERSIGHT OF HIGHER-RISK CONFIDENTIAL SOURCES

EXECUTIVE SUMMARY

I0408347

The Department of Justice (DOJ or Department) Office of the Inspector General (OIG) is conducting an audit of the Drug Enforcement Administration's (DEA) Confidential Source Program. The OIG initiated the audit as a result of the OIG's receipt and review of numerous allegations regarding the DEA's handling and use of confidential sources. This audit report specifically focuses on our examination of the DEA's confidential source policies and their consistency with Department-level standards for law enforcement components, review of the DEA's oversight of certain high-level confidential sources and high-risk activities involving confidential sources, and evaluation of the DEA's administration of death and disability benefits to confidential sources.

Our audit work thus far has been seriously delayed by numerous instances of uncooperativeness from the DEA, including attempts to prohibit the OIG's observation of confidential source file reviews and delays, for months at a time, in providing the OIG with requested confidential source information and documentation. In each instance, the matters were resolved only after the Inspector General elevated them to the DEA Administrator. As a result, over 1 year after we initiated this review, the OIG only has been able to conduct a limited review of the DEA's Confidential Source Program. Nevertheless, we have uncovered several significant issues related to the DEA's management of its Confidential Source Program that we believe require the prompt attention of DOJ and DEA leadership, as identified in this report. We will continue to audit the DEA's Confidential Source Program to more fully assess the DEA's management and oversight of its confidential sources.

The Attorney General's Guidelines Regarding the Use of Confidential Informants (AG Guidelines) provide guidance to all Justice Law Enforcement Agencies(JLEA), including the DEA, related to establishing, approving, utilizing, and evaluating confidential sources.[1] Compliance with the AG Guidelines is important for JLEAs to manage confidential sources appropriately and to mitigate the risks involved with using confidential sources in federal investigations. However, instead of implementing the AG Guidelines verbatim as a separate policy, the DEA chose to incorporate provisions from the AG Guidelines into its preexisting policy – the DEA Special Agents Manual – and the DEA stated that manual successfully captured the

---

[1] The AG Guidelines uses the term "confidential informant," while the DEA uses the term "confidential source." Both terms refer to any individual who provides useful and credible information regarding criminal activities, and from whom the DOJ law enforcement agent expects or intends to obtain additional useful and credible information regarding such activities in the future. For consistency with the DEA, throughout this report we generally use the term "confidential source."

essence of the AG Guidelines. The Criminal Division's leadership approved the DEA policy in January 2004.[2]

We found that the Criminal Division's 2004 approval of the DEA policy allowed the DEA to have a policy that differed in several significant respects from the AG Guidelines' requirements. We believe this has resulted in areas in which the DEA is not fully addressing the concerns underlying the AG Guidelines and, as a result, the DEA's Confidential Source Program lacks sufficient oversight and lacks consistency with the rules governing other DOJ law enforcement components.

The DEA's differing policies have resulted in DEA personnel being able to use high-risk individuals as confidential sources without the level of review as would otherwise be required by the AG Guidelines for high-level and privileged or media-affiliated sources. These categories include individuals who are part of drug trafficking organization leadership, as well as individuals who are lawyers, doctors, or journalists. The AG Guidelines provide a special approval distinction for these individuals because the use of them as confidential sources poses an increased risk to the public and DEA and creates potential legal implications for DOJ. The exemption of the DEA from these requirements results in a relative lack of DEA and DOJ oversight, and in our view should be revisited by the DEA and DOJ.

We similarly found that the DEA policies and practices are not in line with the AG Guidelines' requirements for reviewing, approving, and revoking confidential sources' authorization to conduct Otherwise Illegal Activity (OIA). The effects of inadequate oversight of OIA may not only prove to be detrimental to DEA operations and liability, but also could create unforeseen consequences. For instance, confidential sources may engage in illegal activity that has not been adequately considered, or may overstep their boundaries with a mistaken belief that the DEA sanctions any illegal activities in which they participate. This is another area that should be revisited by the DEA and DOJ.

Moreover, we found that although the DEA's policy includes a provision that generally follows the AG Guidelines requirement for evaluating the use of long-term confidential sources, sources in use for 6 or more consecutive years, the DEA was not adhering to its policy and conducted inadequate and untimely reviews of these sources. In fact, over a 9-year period, DEA documentation indicates that the DEA spent minimal time meeting to determine the appropriateness of the continued use of long term sources. While a more detailed review was done in 2012, and then even more in 2014 (when we observed some of the process) in total we found that the DEA utilized over 240 confidential sources without rigorous review and, in most instances, without the same Departmental concurrence required for other JLEAs. This created a significant risk that improper relationships between government handlers and sources could be allowed to continue over many years, potentially

---

[2] The AG Guidelines' Section I.1 states that upon Attorney General approval of these Guidelines, each JLEA shall develop agency-specific guidelines that comply with the Guidelines, and submit them to the Assistant Attorney General for the Criminal Division for review.

resulting in the divulging of sensitive information or other adverse consequences for the government. In some cases, the DEA continued to use, for up to 6 years without any DOJ intervention, individuals who were involved in unauthorized illegal activities and who were under investigation by federal entities.

We also identified that the DEA's confidential source policies do not include any specific mention of recruiting, establishing, or using sources who are also subject to regulation by the DEA because they have a DEA-provided controlled substance registration number. DOJ guidance emphasizes the need for controls to ensure that no licensee is led to believe that the continued validity of their license is in any way predicated on their status as a source. This was an issue we highlighted in our report on the Bureau of the Alcohol, Tobacco, Firearms and Explosives (ATF) Operation Fast and Furious, where ATF was obtaining information in connection with its criminal investigations from individuals who were also Federal Firearm Licensees.[3] We believe that a clearly stated policy is necessary to provide DEA Special Agents with sufficient information to understand all of the implications of these relationships.

Finally, we learned that the DEA was providing *Federal Employees' Compensation Act* (FECA) benefits to confidential sources, yet had not established a process or any controls regarding the awarding of them.[4] We estimated that, in just the 1-year period from July 1, 2013, through June 30, 2014, the DEA paid 17 confidential sources or their dependents FECA benefits totaling approximately $1.034 million. The DEA lacked a process for thoroughly reviewing FECA claims for confidential sources or determining eligibility for these benefits. In addition, the DEA did not oversee and ensure that the established pay rate for these sources was proper and inappropriately continued using and paying confidential sources who were also receiving full disability payments through FECA. We also found that the DEA had not adequately considered the implications of awarding such benefits on the disclosure obligations of federal prosecutors, and had not consulted the Department about the issue.

As we continue assessing the DEA's Confidential Source Program and get access to more information from the DEA, we expect to conduct in-depth analyses of the types of, payments to, controls over, and use of confidential sources. However, we believe prompt action by the Department and DEA is required to address the issues summarized in this report that directly impact oversight of a highly sensitive and important DEA program. This report makes seven recommendations to the DEA to address the issues we have thus far identified in our review of the DEA's Confidential Source Program.

---

[3] U.S. Department of Justice Office of the Inspector General, *A Review of ATF's Operation Fast and Furious and Related Matters*, (Re-issued November 2012).

[4] *Federal Employees' Compensation Act*, 5 U.S.C. § 8101, et seq. (2011). FECA provides for workers' compensation coverage to federal and U.S. Postal Service workers for injuries or death sustained while in performance of duty.

AUDIT OF THE DRUG ENFORCEMENT ADMINISTRATION'S CONFIDENTIAL SOURCE POLICIES AND OVERSIGHT OF HIGHER-RISK CONFIDENTIAL SOURCES

TABLE OF CONTENTS

AUDIT OF THE DRUG ENFORCEMENT ADMINISTRATION'S CONFIDENTIAL SOURCE POLICIES AND OVERSIGHT OF HIGHER-RISK CONFIDENTIAL SOURCES

The Department of Justice (DOJ) Office of the Inspector General (OIG) is conducting an audit of the Drug Enforcement Administration's (DEA) Confidential Source Program. The OIG initiated the audit as a result of the OIG's receipt and review of numerous allegations regarding the DEA's handling and use of confidential sources. In addition, in 2005, the OIG issued a report on the DEA's payments to confidential sources.[5] The OIG's 2005 report identified needed improvements in the DEA's risk management over the use of and payments to confidential sources.

This audit report specifically focuses on our examination to date of the DEA's confidential source policies and their consistency with Department-level standards for law enforcement components, review of the DEA's oversight of certain high-level confidential sources and high-risk activities involving confidential sources, and evaluation of the DEA's administration of death and disability benefits to confidential sources.

Issues Encountered During this Review

In February 2014, the OIG initiated an audit of the DEA's Confidential Source Program with the preliminary objective of assessing the DEA's management and oversight of its confidential sources. Since that time, the DEA has seriously impeded the OIG's audit process, which has affected our ability to conduct a timely, full, and effective review of the DEA's Confidential Source Program. The DEA made attempts to prohibit the OIG's observation of confidential source file reviews and delayed, for months at a time, the provision of confidential source information and documentation. In these instances, the matters were resolved only after discussions between the Inspector General and the DEA Administrator. As a result, over 1 year after initiating this audit, the OIG has been unable to completely address our original audit objective.

Nevertheless, this audit report identifies certain serious deficiencies in the DEA's management of its confidential source program uncovered thus far during the OIG's initial audit work. The OIG believes these matters require prompt attention from the Department and DEA to address critical issues in this important area of DEA's operations. We will continue to audit the DEA's Confidential Source Program to more fully assess the DEA's management and oversight of its confidential sources.

---

[5] U.S. Department of Justice Office of the Inspector General, *The Drug Enforcement Administration's Payments to Confidential Sources,* (May 2005).

DEA's Confidential Source Program and the Attorney General Guidelines

The DEA defines a confidential source as, "any individual who, with a reasonable expectation of confidentiality, furnishes information regarding drug trafficking, or performs an investigative activity."[6] The DEA's policy stipulates that every confidential source must act under the direction and control of DEA Controlling/Supervisory personnel when performing an investigative activity. According to DEA officials, confidential sources are a critical part of its law enforcement operations, referring to them as the "bread and butter" of the agency. Nevertheless, DEA and DOJ officials have acknowledged that there are risks involved with using confidential sources because these individuals often have criminal backgrounds and offer their assistance or cooperation in return for cash or consideration for a reduced criminal sentence. Therefore, the utilization of confidential sources requires significant oversight and attentive program management.

Although the DEA generally relies on its field office personnel to manage, direct, and evaluate the use of confidential sources, the DEA's Confidential Source Unit is the headquarters entity responsible for the oversight of all confidential source-related matters. The Confidential Source Unit provides support to the field and manages the electronic system, Confidential Source System Concorde (CSSC), which contains data on each source. In addition, the Confidential Source Unit updates and implements DEA confidential source policies, which are prescribed in section 6612 of the DEA Special Agents Manual. This section of the Agents Manual, entitled, "Confidential Sources," contains the mandatory requirements for the DEA's Confidential Source Program and the conditions for establishing, using, and reviewing confidential sources.

The Attorney General's Guidelines Regarding the Use of Confidential Informants (AG Guidelines) provide guidance and requirements to all Justice Law Enforcement Agencies (JLEAs), including the DEA, related to establishing, approving, utilizing, and evaluating a confidential source.[7] In 2001 and again later in 2002, DOJ updated the AG Guidelines to address mismanagement, misconduct, and criminal prosecution issues related to the handling of confidential sources; and to enhance DOJ oversight of JLEAs' use of confidential sources. AG Guidelines' Section I.1 states that each JLEA shall develop agency-specific guidelines that comply with the AG Guidelines and submit those agency-specific guidelines to the Assistant Attorney General for the Criminal Division for review.

---

[6] DEA Special Agents Manual, Section 6612.11, A.

[7] The AG Guidelines uses the term "confidential informant," while the DEA uses the term "confidential source." Both terms refer to any individual who provides useful and credible information to a DOJ law enforcement agent regarding criminal activities, and from whom the DOJ law enforcement agent expects or intends to obtain additional useful and credible information regarding such activities in the future. For consistency with the DEA, throughout this report we generally use the term "confidential source."

Criminal Division Approval of the DEA Policy

Between 2001 and 2004, DOJ's Criminal Division reviewed the DEA's confidential source policies to ensure that they complied with the AG Guidelines. According to historical documents that were provided to the OIG during our 2005 audit noted above, the DOJ representatives who were involved in the review of the DEA's policies included an Assistant United States Attorney (AUSA) and the following Criminal Division officials: the Assistant Attorney General, two Deputy Assistant Attorneys General (DAAG), the Deputy Chief of the Organized Crime and Racketeering Section, and the Principal Deputy for the Narcotics and Dangerous Drugs Section. The documents indicate that the various officials had differing opinions on whether the DEA's policies complied with the AG Guidelines.

In a memorandum dated August 6, 2001, one of the DAAGs indicated support for the DEA's confidential source policies as written in the DEA Special Agents Manual. By contrast, a September 3, 2002, memorandum from the AUSA and the Deputy Chief of the Criminal Division's Organized Crime and Racketeering Section identified numerous significant deviations between the DEA's policy and the AG Guidelines. In addition, the memorandum stated that the DEA's Confidential Source Program policies were difficult to follow because instead of implementing the AG Guidelines verbatim as a separate policy, the DEA chose to incorporate provisions from the AG Guidelines into its preexisting policy – the DEA Special Agents Manual.

In a September 26, 2002, Criminal Division memorandum responding to this evaluation, the Principal Deputy for the Criminal Division's Narcotics and Drugs Section and the DAAG who authored the August 6, 2001, memorandum stated that the language in the AG Guidelines was a foreign vocabulary and structure to DEA personnel and that it did not cover all aspects of the DEA's confidential source handling. In this memorandum, these two Criminal Division officials reasoned that in order to ensure that DEA Special Agents understood the AG Guidelines' requirements and implemented them, the DEA needed to integrate the requirements into its DEA Special Agents Manual, which was "written from beginning to end by DEA for DEA." These Criminal Division officials further stated that the DEA had "successfully captured the spirit and essence of the AG Guidelines in the DEA Special Agents Manual."

Various Criminal Division documents indicate that between September 2002 and January 2004, numerous meetings were held to discuss the varying Criminal Division opinions on the DEA's policy, its compliance with the AG Guidelines, and specific areas of disagreement. The documents also indicate that the DEA made revisions to certain provisions of its Special Agents Manual. The Criminal Division's leadership subsequently approved the DEA's policy on January 8, 2004. The memorandum documenting the Criminal Division's approval of the DEA's policy states "...the Criminal Division finds that the DEA [Special] Agents Manual fully complies with the Attorney General's Guidelines..."

However, we found that DEA's policy changes did not take into account all of the inconsistencies between the DEA policy and the AG Guidelines. Moreover, the memorandum did not cite the AG Guidelines' provision that allowed for exceptions to compliance with those policies. The OIG believes that the Criminal Division's 2004 approval of the DEA policy allowed the DEA to have a policy that differed in several significant respects from the AG Guidelines' requirements, such as policies and practices for establishing and approving certain confidential sources and for utilizing sources to undertake high-risk activities. We believe that this has resulted in areas in which the DEA is not fully addressing the concerns underlying the AG Guidelines and, as a result, the DEA's Confidential Source Program lacks sufficient oversight. Moreover, the DEA's policies lack consistency with the rules governing other DOJ law enforcement components and this undermines the intent of a uniform set of guidelines for all DOJ law enforcement components.

Confidential Source Categories

One area in which the DEA Special Agents Manual and the AG Guidelines are not consistent is in the identification and definition of categories of confidential sources. As illustrated in Table 1, the AG Guidelines identify three types of confidential sources and six sub-categories of confidential sources that are specifically identified because they require additional scrutiny and special approval.

Table 1

AG Guidelines' Categories of Confidential Informants

Categories	Definition
Confidential Informant	Any individual who provides useful and credible information to a JLEA regarding felonious criminal activities, and from whom the JLEA expects or intends to obtain additional useful and credible information regarding such activities in the future.
Cooperating Defendant/ Witness	A confidential informant who has agreed to testify in a proceeding as a result of having provided information to the JLEA; and is a defendant or potential witness who has a written agreement with a federal prosecutor, pursuant to which the individual has an expectation of future judicial or prosecutorial consideration or assistance as a result of having provided information to the JLEA, or is a potential witness who has had a federal prosecutor concurs in all material aspects of his or her use by the JLEA.
Source of Information	A confidential informant who provides information to a JLEA solely as a result of legitimate routine access to information or records and not as a result of criminal association with persons of investigative interest to the JLEA.
Sub-Categories	**Definition and Special Approval Requirements**
High Level	A confidential informant who is part of the senior leadership of an enterprise that has a national or international sphere of activities, or high significance to the JLEA's national objectives, even if the enterprise's sphere of activities is local or regional; and engages in, or uses others to commit, any conduct described as Tier 1 Otherwise Illegal Activity (OIA).[8] Registration or establishment requires approval from an oversight committee, referred to as the Confidential Informant Review Committee (CIRC), which includes representatives from the JLEA and DOJ.[9]
Privileged or Media-Related	An individual who is under obligation of legal privilege of confidentiality (such as doctors, lawyers, and clergy) or who is affiliated with the news media. Registration or establishment requires approval from the CIRC.
Long-term	Any individual who has been registered as an informant for more than six consecutive years. The CIRC must review and approve continued use of these informants.
Individuals in Custody	Any individual who is a federal, state, or local prisoner, probationer, parolee, detainee, and on supervised release. Registration or establishment requires approval from the Criminal Division.
WITSEC Participant	Any individual who is a current or former participant in the Federal Witness Security Program. Registration or establishment requires approval from the Criminal Division and the United States Marshals Service.
Fugitive	An individual for whom a federal, state, or local law enforcement agency has placed a wanted record in the National Crime Information Center (NCIC); who is located either within the US or in a country with which the US has an extradition treaty; and who the law enforcement agency that has placed the wanted record in the NCIC is willing to take into custody upon his or her arrest and, if necessary, seek his or her extradition to its jurisdiction. A JLEA shall have no communication with a fugitive unless the JLEA receives approval from the law enforcement agency and FPO for the District issuing the warrant or if the purpose of communication is to arrest the fugitive.

Source: The AG Guidelines

---

[8] Section IB.10 of the AG Guidelines defines Tier 1 OIA. We provide a more detailed definition of and a more in-depth examination of Tier 1 OIA in the Authorization of OIA section of this report.

[9] The AG Guidelines defines the initial stage of confidential source suitability determination and review as registration, while the DEA refers to this stage as establishment. Throughout the report, we generally use the DEA's terminology of establishment to convey the initial suitability and review process.

The DEA identifies multiple categories of confidential sources, as described in Table 2.

Table 2

Overview of DEA Confidential Source Categories

Categories[10]	Definitions and Approvals
Restricted Use	A confidential source who will be subject to a greater degree of supervisory control based upon factors within his/her background that indicates a need for such supervision.
Defendant	A confidential source who was under arrest or is subject to arrest and prosecution for a federal or state offense; requires federal or state prosecutor concurrence for establishment.
Protected Name	An individual whose public identification or utilization as a DEA confidential source could pose a threat to the national security of the United States or a foreign country, or result in a high likelihood of violence to the confidential source and/or his/her family members or associates, or is likely to raise complex legal issues.
Regular Use	A confidential source who does not meet the criteria for establishment as a Restricted Use, Defendant, or Protected Name confidential source.
Limited Use	An individual established as a confidential source for payment purposes only and who is a "professional" business person or a "tipster."

Source: DEA

A comparison of the preceding tables demonstrates that the DEA's confidential source categories do not specifically correlate to the categories established in the AG Guidelines, which makes it more difficult to ensure that the DEA is following the same requirements for each confidential source category that are imposed on other JLEAs. Moreover, the DEA's Confidential Source Unit does not have any documentation that shows how the DEA's confidential source categories correlate to the AG Guidelines' source categories. At the OIG's request, the DEA created a cross-walk between its confidential source categories and the AG Guidelines categories, which is included in Appendix 1. We found that this cross-walk provided a correlation between some of the confidential source categories, such as the DEA's Defendant category corresponding to the AG Guidelines' Cooperating Defendant/Witness category and the DEA's Limited Use category corresponding to the AG Guidelines' Source of Information category. However, the correlation still did not account for specific requirements of the AG Guidelines, including the establishment of special approval confidential sources, as described in the following section.

Confidential Sources Requiring Special Approval

According to documents supporting the Criminal Division's review of the DEA confidential source policies, the requirement for an oversight committee is one of the most important provisions of the AG Guidelines. The AG Guidelines require the JLEA to establish a Confidential Informant Review Committee (CIRC) for the purposes of reviewing certain decisions relating to the registration and utilization of

---

[10] The DEA does not have a unique category for long-term confidential sources, but it does use this term (outside of its Special Agents Manual) and identifies these individuals as sources active for 6 or more consecutive years.

confidential informants. According to the AG Guidelines, the CIRC will include specific representatives of the JLEA, as well as a Criminal Division representative and an Assistant United States Attorney (AUSA). Along with other matters, the CIRC is required to review the establishment and approve the use of confidential sources who present greater risks of potential liability, intrusion into governmental processes, and other adverse consequences. These confidential sources fall into the AG Guidelines' three special approval sub-categories: (1) high-level confidential sources; (2) privileged or media-affiliated confidential sources, such as lawyers, doctors, and journalists; and (3) long-term confidential sources.

The DEA has identified its Sensitive Activity Review Committee (SARC) as its established committee for conducting the CIRC-related responsibilities identified in the AG Guidelines. According to the DEA Special Agents Manual, the SARC is composed of DEA's Chief of Global Enforcement, Chief Counsel, appropriate Office of Global Enforcement Section Chief(s), the Chief of the Undercover and Sensitive Investigations Section, relevant Special Agents in Charge or Regional Directors and case agents responsible for matters before the SARC, and a DOJ representative. The DEA's Office of Undercover and Sensitive Investigations is responsible for managing and administering all SARC-related activities. Under DEA's policy, the SARC is responsible for examining certain operational proposals to ensure the plans for proposed sensitive investigative activities are well-founded and all issues of concern are sufficiently addressed.

However, the DEA's policy defining the SARC does not identify any specific position or individual for the DOJ representative(s), or, as directed by the AG Guidelines, if the DOJ representatives include a Deputy Assistant Attorney General for the Criminal Division and an Assistant United States Attorney (AUSA). In addition, we found that Criminal Division-approved DEA policy does not require the SARC to approve the establishment and use of what are categorized as high-level or privileged confidential sources under the AG Guidelines, and that the SARC does not undertake such a review and approval. The lack of DEA oversight over such confidential sources is troubling given the assessment reflected in the AG Guidelines that these categories of confidential sources pose the greatest risk to the U.S. government and the public. In addition, although DEA policy includes provisions regarding SARC review of long-term confidential sources, and these provisions are generally consistent with the AG Guidelines, we found myriad issues related to the implementation of this requirement, which are discussed later in the report.

High-Level Confidential Sources

The DEA does not use the term "high level" to identify any of its confidential sources and does not have a policy, as required under the AG Guidelines that covers the establishment and use of an individual who fits the AG Guidelines' definition of a high-level confidential source. Further, prior to creating one at the OIG's request, the DEA did not have a cross-walk or any other document correlating the DEA confidential source categories and the AG Guidelines' high-level confidential source category.

DEA officials stated that individual confidential sources categorized by the DEA as Restricted-Use, Protected Name, Defendant, or Regular-Use could potentially correspond to the AG Guidelines' high-level category, but this categorization is entirely dependent on what happens during an investigation and is not based upon the characteristics of a confidential source. Therefore, the DEA would apply its normal establishment procedures when initially recruiting a high-level confidential source, and DEA policy has no provisions for SARC involvement in any type of confidential source establishment. By contrast, the AG Guidelines are clear that an individual who meets the criteria for a high-level confidential source should be reviewed by the CIRC, which would include DOJ Criminal Division and U.S. Attorney's Office consideration, before receiving approval to be established as a confidential source.

According to DEA officials, the DEA targets the senior leadership of drug organizations and, therefore, if such an individual became a confidential source then the person would be defined as a Defendant confidential source because they were subject to arrest and prosecution, and would necessarily require the approval of a prosecutor. Therefore, the category of high level is not needed. However, the requirement to consider such individuals as Defendant confidential sources is not included in the DEA's Special Agent Manual, and we did not identify any documentation where this policy was conveyed to DEA Special Agents.

Moreover, when we asked another DEA official if the DEA had a SARC approval requirement for establishing a high-level confidential source, this official explained that the DEA does not have any confidential sources who fit the definition of the high-level category identified in the AG Guidelines. This explanation is contrary to the aforementioned statement that alluded to the DEA's use of what would otherwise be considered high-level confidential sources under the rubric of Defendant confidential sources.

The lack of explicit DEA policy and inconsistent treatment of what would be high-level confidential sources under the AG Guidelines increases the risk that the DEA is using what would otherwise be considered as high-level sources without sufficient oversight. The AG Guidelines reflect that the use of high-level sources comes at a risk to the U.S. government and the public because these individuals are associated with and may be directing the activities of criminal organizations. Therefore, by approving a policy that does not comply with the AG Guidelines' requirements related to high-level sources, the Department has allowed the DEA to have a policy that does not incorporate appropriate safeguards and necessary scrutiny of the risk and reward of using such individuals as confidential sources.

Privileged or Media-Affiliated Confidential Sources

As previously noted, the AG Guidelines require that a case agent first obtain the written approval of the CIRC prior to utilizing as a confidential source an individual who is under the obligation of a legal privilege of confidentiality or affiliated with the media. The DEA Special Agents Manual states that any individual who is a public official, a representative of the news media, or a party to privileged communications (e.g., a member of the clergy, physician, lawyer, etc.) should be categorized as a Protected Name confidential source. DEA policy requires a Senior Executive Service (SES) manager within the DEA to authorize the use of a Protected Name confidential source by a domestic field office. However, this level of approval differs markedly from the AG Guidelines' requirement for CIRC approval of all privileged and media-affiliated confidential sources, which includes consideration by high-level agency headquarters officials, the Criminal Division, and an AUSA. Although the DEA's policy does require SARC approval for the use of a confidential source acting in an undercover capacity who will "request information from an attorney, physician, clergyman, or member of the news media about a matter or person that would be considered privileged," it does not provide for the SARC review for the establishment of an individual who otherwise fits the criteria of a privileged or media-affiliated confidential source.

Moreover, various DEA headquarters officials related to us disparate practices for the establishment of privileged or media-affiliated confidential sources. Specifically, some DEA headquarters officials stated that Special Agents would not establish as a confidential source or utilize an individual for information associated with their privileged or media-related status. Other DEA headquarters' officials acknowledged that Special Agents are permitted to establish as a confidential source a privileged or media-affiliated status individual, such as a doctor or lawyer, to obtain information not related to the source's employment. In these cases, the DEA's legal staff would review the proposed utilization of the privileged or media-affiliated individual to ensure there is not a breach of privilege. However, this requirement and process is not included in the DEA Special Agents Manual section on confidential sources. Thus, the DEA solely relies on the discretion and judgment of its special agents to identify occupations that necessitate additional review and seek that from DEA legal staff. In addition, should that process occur, it would still be inconsistent with the heightened level of independent review for the establishment of sources in such sensitive occupations, as required for other DOJ law enforcement components under the AG Guidelines.

During our limited review of confidential source files, we identified two DEA confidential sources who were attorneys.[11] Despite these individuals' privileged status, the confidential source files did not contain any documentation indicating that the DEA's legal staff had reviewed the establishment of the confidential source or that the confidential sources were ever categorized as Protected Name confidential sources because they were parties to protected communications. Neither of these confidential source files contained any documentation reflecting Special Agent in Charge (SAC) or other Senior Executive Service-level approval, much less SARC review and approval.

---

[11] Although our limited review of confidential source files did not reveal any confidential sources who held media-related positions, the potential exists that these same failures have occurred for individuals who qualify for this special approval category.

We believe that the DEA's policy and practice regarding the establishment of privileged or media-related confidential sources do not reflect appropriate consideration of the potential risks associated with these confidential sources.

Authorization of Otherwise Illegal Activity

The AG Guidelines provide for JLEAs to authorize confidential sources to engage in activity that would otherwise be illegal if they were not acting under the direction of the government. This is referred to in the AG Guidelines as Otherwise Illegal Activity (OIA) and there are two types – Tier 1 OIA and Tier 2 OIA. More serious offenses are categorized as Tier 1 OIA, and involve the commission or the significant risk of the commission of certain offenses, including acts of violence; corrupt conduct by senior federal, state, or local public officials; or the manufacturing, importing, exporting, possession, or trafficking in what would be considered as large quantities of controlled substances under the federal sentencing guidelines.[12] Tier 2 OIA is defined as any other activity that would constitute a misdemeanor or felony under federal, state, or local law if engaged in by a person acting without authorization.

The AG Guidelines mandate that Tier 1 OIA be authorized in advance and in writing for a specified period, not to exceed 90 days, by the agency's Special Agent in Charge and the appropriate Chief Federal Prosecutor.[13] Tier 2 OIA can be approved at a lower level, namely by an agency's senior field office manager, which could be an Assistant Special Agent in Charge. The management of OIA as it relates to confidential sources requires careful consideration and the AG Guidelines outline clear instructions for agencies that direct confidential sources to perform OIA. Figure 1 provides an overview of these instructions, which include obtaining specific approval and documenting in a confidential source's file: (1) the approval, (2) the instructions provided to the source, (3) the source's acknowledgement of the instructions received, and (4) the revocation of the authorization.

---

[12] See United States Sentencing Guidelines § 2D1.1(c)(1). The following provide an overview of drug quantities that would meet this threshold under the sentencing guidelines: 90 kilograms or more of heroin; 450 kilograms or more of cocaine; 25.2 kilograms or more of cocaine base; 45 kilograms or more of methamphetamine; and 90,000 kilograms or more of marijuana.

[13] The AG Guidelines define the Chief Federal Prosecutor as the head of a Federal Prosecuting Office, including the United States Attorneys' Offices; the Criminal Division, Tax Division, Civil Rights Division, Antitrust Division, and Environment and Natural Resources Division of the Department of Justice; or any other litigating component of the Department of Justice with authority to prosecute federal criminal offenses.

Figure 1

AG Guidelines Requirements for
Authorization and Management of Confidential Sources Performing OIA

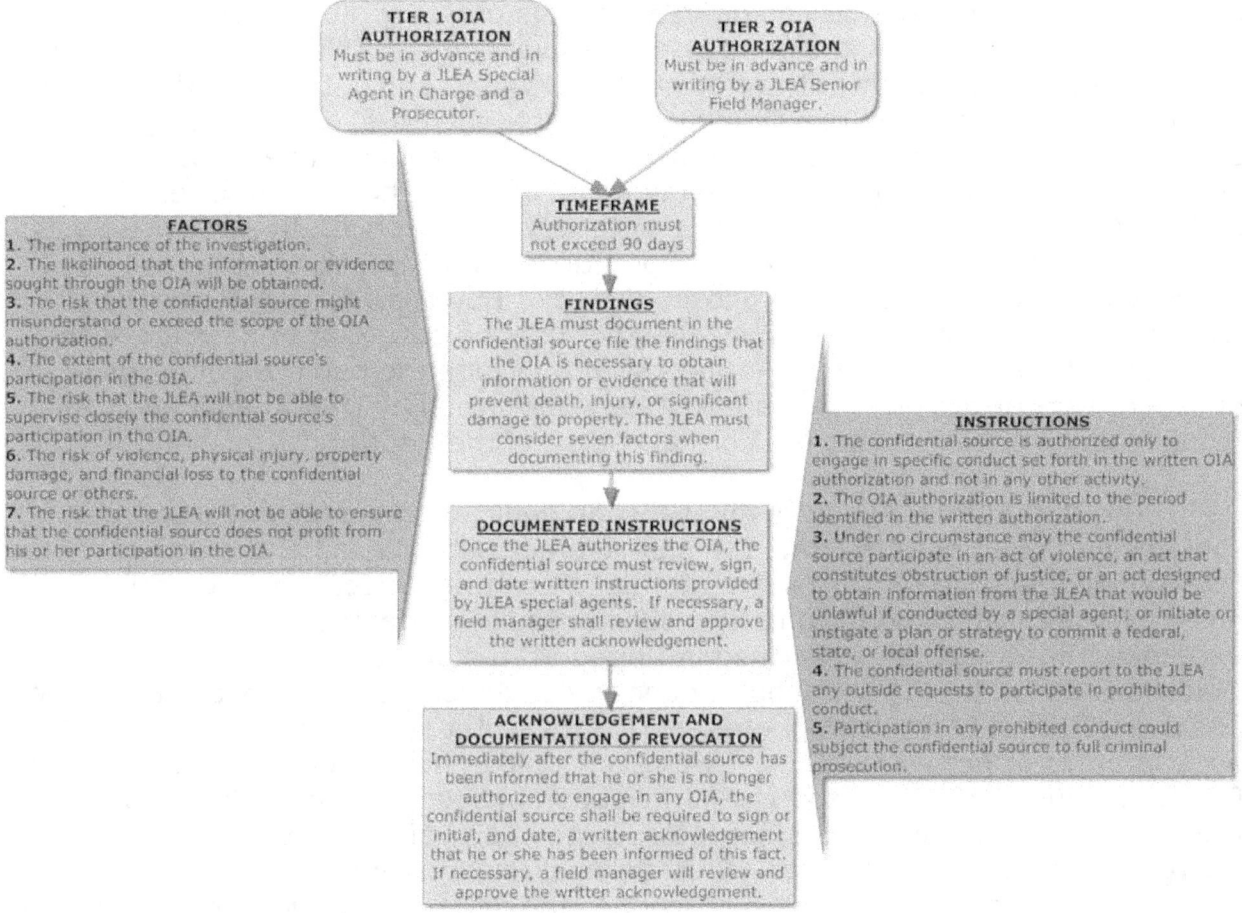

Source: The AG Guidelines

As discussed above, the Criminal Division had reviewed the DEA Special Agents Manual for compliance with the AG Guidelines and formally approved the DEA's policy in 2004. An August 6, 2001, memorandum from a DAAG for the Criminal Division states that because, "the DEA's policy requires that all cases involving illegal activity on the part of an informant be thoroughly discussed with the FPO [Federal Prosecuting Official], the DEA does not anticipate utilizing a source as a "confidential informant" as defined by the [AG] Guidelines." In addition, the DAAG's memorandum stated that the DEA had made efforts to minimize any adverse effects of confidential source participation in OIA, including: (1) requiring confidential sources to annually sign a form restricting the source from participating in unauthorized unlawful acts; and (2) requiring controlling investigators to provide specific instructions regarding the confidential source's participation in each stage of an investigation.

11

We reviewed DEA policy documents for references to OIA and how the DEA handles such sensitive activities, especially when it involves confidential sources. The DEA Special Agents Manual has a specific section dedicated to sensitive investigative activities and this section contains a list of 18 sensitive operations and the requirements for getting these operations approved. This list includes activities that "will involve the commission of an act that is proscribed by federal, state, or local law as a felony or that is otherwise a serious crime." This entry would appear to be somewhat consistent with what would fall within either Tier 1 or Tier 2 of the AG Guidelines. Generally, this DEA policy requires the listed activities to go through a formal approval process that includes high-level DEA headquarters officials from the Office of Global Enforcement, Office of the Chief of Operations, and the Chief Counsel's office, and U.S. Attorney concurrence. In some instances, at the discretion of the DEA's Chief of Operations Enforcement, the DEA will convene a SARC to review the proposed activity. However, for any instances of "sensitive activity," the DEA manual does not use the term OIA to describe such conduct and the manual notes: "This does not include the purchase of drugs or other undercover activities that are routinely performed by DEA Agents and CSs [confidential sources] during the normal course of their duties."

The DEA Special Agents Manual section dedicated to confidential sources contains two references to OIA. The first reference stipulates: If the activity of the CS [confidential source] will involve the manufacturing, importing, exporting, possession, or trafficking of controlled substances in a quantity equal to or exceeding those quantities specified in United States Sentencing Guidelines 2D1.1 (c) (1), it cannot, under any circumstances, proceed without the prior concurrence of an appropriate federal prosecutor regarding all material aspects of his or her use by DEA.[14] However, unlike the AG Guidelines' requirement for authorizing confidential sources participation in such large quantity drug trafficking, the DEA policy does not incorporate approval by the Special Agent in Charge and does not track other AG Guidelines' requirements for the OIA process, including documenting findings, instructions, and acknowledgement of revocation of OIA authorization. In addition, the DEA policy does not reach smaller quantity drug offense involvement that would otherwise come within Tier 2 OIA under the AG Guidelines.

The second reference to OIA in the confidential source section of the Special Agents Manual requires DEA Supervisory Special Agents, during their quarterly review of confidential source files, to assess sources' continued engagement in OIA."[15] However, this section of the DEA Special Agents Manual does not provide further detail for how the DEA initially approves the use of confidential sources in OIA and contains no cross-reference to the Special Agents Manual section on sensitive activities mentioned above. Moreover, the DEA's requirements for

---

[14] This requirement is the one referenced in the 2001 Criminal Division memorandum of the DEA's policies discussed following Figure 1, and tracks the AG Guidelines' definition of Tier 1 OIA involving large quantity drug trafficking as detailed in footnote 12.

[15] DEA Special Agents Manual, Section 6612.6 B5.

supervisory quarterly reviews of confidential source files, as referenced in the policy information above, are no longer in effect.[16]

Because the DEA Special Agents Manual section on sensitive activities explicitly excludes drug buys and other routine confidential source activities, and the DEA Special Agents Manual section on confidential sources does not provide detail on the process for using confidential sources to perform illegal acts such as drug buys, does not require SAC approval for larger drug deals, and does not reach smaller ones, we believe that DEA's official policies do not sufficiently address the concerns underlying the otherwise applicable AG Guidelines requirements for approving the use of confidential sources in Tier 1 and 2 OIA.

Because of the lack of detail in the DEA's formal policies addressing OIA, we asked DEA officials to explain the process for reviewing, approving, and revoking DEA authorization for confidential sources to participate in activities that would constitute OIA. In response, we were provided several differing explanations. Initially, we were told by a DEA official that the DEA does not authorize any type of OIA. Subsequently, the OIG was told that the purchase of drugs or other undercover activities that are routinely performed by DEA Special Agents and confidential sources during the normal course of their duties are activities performed under the legal authority granted to DEA under Title 21.[17] Still other DEA officials told us that prior to utilizing a confidential source in an operation (including a drug buy), Special Agents prepare a written operations plan and submit it to senior field division officials for approval.

Of all the information we were provided, the DEA's use and approval of written Operations Plans seemed to provide the closest comparison to the requirements of the AG Guidelines. However, neither the DEA Special Agents Manual section devoted to confidential sources nor the one devoted to sensitive investigative activity included instructions for the preparation, approval, or documentation of an operations plan. Further, during our limited review of confidential source files we did not identify any files that included documentation of authorization for the confidential source to conduct narcotics-related OIA. As such, we looked for evidence of approved operations plans in two investigative case files referred to in two confidential sources' files as cases involving confidential sources performing OIA. We found that one investigative case file contained operations plans and one did not. When we reviewed the operations plans in the one investigative case file, we found that one plan did not contain approval signatures. Although not required under DEA policy, we also examined the files for any indication that the AG Guidelines requirements for OIA may have been otherwise fulfilled. We found no evidence in any files that DEA confidential sources were made aware of or signed acknowledgement of rules specific to OIA and there was

---

[16] In 2007, the DEA eliminated the requirement for quarterly supervisory reviews of confidential source files because it was seen as redundant to a different DEA policy that requires supervisory agents to participate in a quarterly debriefing with each confidential source.

[17] *The Controlled Substances Act.* 21 U.S.C. § 801 (2012).

no indication that the confidential sources were informed of their responsibilities, limitations, or revocation of authority to perform OIA.[18]

We believe the DEA's policies do not adequately address the concerns and risks involved in authorizing confidential sources to conduct and participate in OIA and do not correspond to the AG Guidelines' requirements in place to mitigate these risks. Moreover, because OIA is not comprehensively addressed in the DEA policies regarding sensitive circumstances or confidential sources, DEA personnel do not appear to have a solid understanding of OIA, or the expectations for DEA's procedures that involve OIA. Further, the fact that the DEA confidential source files we reviewed did not contain documentation authorizing the confidential source to conduct narcotics-related OIA limits supervision and oversight of these activities. These inadequate DEA policies and procedures related to OIA greatly increase the risk to the DEA, the U.S. government, and the public from the involvement of DEA confidential sources in OIA. DEA confidential sources could engage in illegal activity that has not been adequately considered, or become involved in additional illegal activities beyond those that have been considered with the mistaken belief that they are doing so with the authorization of the DEA. Further, an ill-considered or unclear decision to authorize a confidential source to engage in OIA may create significant difficulties in prosecuting the source or co-conspirators on charges related to the source's activities.

Review of Long-Term Confidential Sources

Under the AG Guidelines, the Confidential Informant Review Committee (CIRC) must approve the continued use of each confidential source who has been registered for more than 6 consecutive years. Such sources are referred to under the AG Guidelines as long-term sources. According to a DOJ official, this requirement was included in the AG Guidelines due to concerns over a government handler and a source developing an inappropriate relationship. This may involve the government handler becoming so close to the source that the handler improperly divulges information to the source, or result in other adverse consequences for the government. Requiring review of long-term sources mitigates the risk that such a relationship might develop and go unnoticed and ensures that the continued use of such long-term sources is warranted and handled appropriately.

The AG Guidelines stipulate that when a confidential source reaches the 6 consecutive year threshold and, to the extent the source remains open, every 6 years thereafter, the CIRC shall convene to review the confidential source's completed Initial and Continuing Suitability Reports and Recommendations and decide whether, and under what conditions, the agency should continue to utilize the individual as a confidential source. The AG Guidelines stipulate that a CIRC

---

[18] All DEA confidential sources are required to sign a form each year acknowledging that they are not allowed to take part in any illegal activity not specifically approved by a prosecutor or the controlling agent. However, this is a standard form that all sources are required to sign and is not specific to any individual operations or activities.

include an agency official at or above the Deputy Assistant Director level, a Deputy Assistant Attorney for the Criminal Division (DAAG), and an Assistant United States Attorney (AUSA).

Although the DEA Special Agents Manual does not use the term "long-term," it includes a requirement for the SARC to review domestic confidential sources who have been continuously in an active status for 6 years, and who are to remain in an active status. The DEA Special Agents Manual stipulates that the DEA's Confidential Source Unit and Office for Undercover and Sensitive Investigations should coordinate to ensure that the SARC reviews the confidential source files to determine if a confidential source should remain in an active status. During the OIG's prior review of the DEA's Confidential Source Program, we found deficiencies in the DEA's process for reviewing long-term confidential sources. In response to the OIG's report, the DEA provided updated guidance to reinforce the DEA's requirement to provide a thorough examination of risk assessment factors and relevant paperwork related to the establishment and suitability of long-term confidential sources. However, during this audit the OIG found that the reviews performed by the DEA SARC for the continued use of long-term confidential sources were both deficient and untimely.

Inadequate SARC Review

Based on the aforementioned risks involved with long-term sources, the oversight of these long-term confidential sources is critical to the overall management of the DEA's Confidential Source Program. Further, the importance of the long-term confidential source reviews requires that the SARC members, including any DOJ representatives, invest an appropriate amount of time and effort evaluating the benefits and risks of the continued use of each long-term confidential source.

We reviewed the DEA's documented meeting minutes for the SARC meetings conducted specifically for the review of long-term confidential sources that occurred between 2003 and 2012 and found that between 2003 and 2012, the DEA SARC's reviews of long-term confidential sources appear to have been inadequate and infrequent. The DEA held only 7 SARC meetings during that 9-year period. Moreover, between its meeting in October 2009 and its most recent meeting in July 2014, a nearly 5-year timespan, the SARC met only once, in February 2012.

Each set of meeting minutes we reviewed briefly and broadly described the SARC's review of long-term confidential sources. The minutes also identified the time of day that the meetings started and ended, as well as the number of sources reviewed. Our review of the minutes indicates that certain information obtained from Special Agents in Charge of field offices using the long-term confidential sources was provided to SARC members. This information included the date of activation in the particular office, confidential source type, information on adverse performance/behavior, a dollar amount identified as the total amount of lifetime payments received, any judicial considerations given, a brief synopsis of accomplishments, and justification for continued status. It appears from the meeting minutes that DEA headquarters officials compiled this information into a listing [spreadsheet] and provided it to the SARC members prior to the formal meetings. Prior to 2006, the meeting minutes make no reference to confidential source files or information equivalent to the Establishment and Continuing Suitability Reports and Recommendations forms, which is the minimum requirement set forth by the AG Guidelines for other JLEAs. Although the minutes reflect that starting in 2006, headquarters' confidential source files were available for SARC members during the formal meetings, there is no indication that any SARC members actually reviewed any of these files. According to this information, between 2003 and 2012, during these formal meetings the SARC devoted what we calculated to be an average of just 1 minute per confidential source to consider the appropriateness of the source's continued use.

Our review of historical SARC events also revealed that despite the DEA Special Agents Manual requirement that DOJ representative(s) participate in SARC meetings, in some instances the DEA convened SARC meetings without any DOJ representatives present. As shown in Table 3, neither a DAAG nor an AUSA were present at two of the seven meetings.[19] In addition, there was only one SARC meeting between 2003 and 2012 in which both an AUSA and Criminal Division representative were in attendance for the review of long-term confidential sources, which is what is required by the AG Guidelines. Thus, in these instances, the DEA failed to ensure that 249 long-term DEA confidential sources received the same external DOJ oversight provided to other JLEAs' long-term confidential sources.

---

[19] The 2004 minutes state that the Criminal Division official was unable to attend the meeting; however, she concurred with the list and had no issues to report. In addition, the 2007 minutes state that the Criminal Division official was absent from the meeting, had previously been sent the confidential source spreadsheet and all existing information regarding the confidential sources subject to review, and had not contacted the DEA regarding any questions or concerns relative to any of the confidential sources.

Table 3

**Overview of SARC Reviews of Long-term Confidential Sources
2003 through 2012**

	Meeting Date	Sources Reviewed	Meeting Length (in minutes)	Calculated Average Time Reviewing Each Confidential Source (in minutes and seconds)	External Participation	
					Criminal Division DAAG	AUSA
1	11/13/2003	48	20	25 seconds	YES	NO
2	11/04/2004	60	15	15 seconds	NO	NO
3	01/31/2006	67	15	13 seconds	YES	NO
4	04/26/2007	16	40	2 minutes and 30 seconds	NO	NO
5	05/13/2008	30	15	30 seconds	YES	NO
6	10/27/2009	28	15	32 seconds	YES	NO
7	02/29/2012	25	150	6 minutes	YES	YES

Source: OIG analysis of DEA documentation

It is noteworthy that the DEA spent significantly more time reviewing the long-term confidential source information during the 2012 SARC meeting and, based on the meeting minutes and our review of DEA documentation, as well as interviews with DEA officials, this is the year the DEA established specific files for the SARC review, as discussed below. These files provided information from the official confidential source files to the SARC, in addition to the Special Agent in Charge's testament of confidential source information. DEA officials and a Criminal Division official attributed these changes to the involvement of new SARC leadership at DEA and a change in the participating DOJ officials. However, our review of the SARC files for the 2012 meeting revealed that the files did not contain basic information such as the annual forms documenting the DEA's assessment of the sources' continued suitability (DEA Form 512b) for each of the 6 years under review, identification of DEA offices concurrently using the sources, or criminal history reports. In addition, based on our review of the meeting minutes, the SARC members generally relied on the Confidential Source Unit's review of the confidential source documentation and Special Agent in Charge testimonial to inform their decisions to concur with the continued use of long-term confidential source up for review. This conclusion was substantiated by at least one DEA staff member who attended the 2012 meeting told us that not every SARC member reviewed all of the confidential source files or critically reviewed the continued use of each source but, rather, the SARC allowed certain DEA officials to attest to the appropriateness of the continued use of long-term confidential sources. We therefore concluded that all of the SARC reviews from 2003 through 2012 did not fully satisfy the intent of the AG Guidelines requirements for additional scrutiny and oversight of long-term confidential sources.

2014 SARC Meeting and Confidential File Preparation

After initiating our audit, we inquired about the possibility of observing a DEA SARC meeting for the review of long-term confidential sources. We were informed that a meeting would be held on June 20, 2014. We were also informed that this SARC meeting represented the DEA's review of long-term sources who had reached the 6-year threshold by January 2013, and that the DEA had originally expected for the meeting to occur in 2013. However, the meeting did not occur as expected due to scheduling issues and conflicts with the required participants.

The meeting was then subsequently postponed twice, on June 20, 2014, and July 1, 2014, while discussions were held between OIG, DEA, and Criminal Division leadership about the OIG's attendance at the meeting. On July 8, 2014, OIG, DEA, and Criminal Division leadership officials agreed that OIG representatives would be in attendance for an agreed-upon portion of the meeting, which was subsequently scheduled for July 18, 2014.[20]

At the July 18, 2014, SARC meeting, the DAAG and AUSA asked questions pertaining to general DEA Confidential Source Program requirements and DEA processes for documenting information. The DAAG and AUSA initiated their review of an individual long-term confidential source by selecting it from a list and retrieving a paper file from a stack that the DEA had made available in its meeting room. Upon taking time to review information in the file at the meeting, the DAAG and AUSA then asked specific questions pertaining to information in the file, such as criminal history entries or payments received. As a result, the SARC only fully reviewed two files over a 2-hour period and the meeting was carried over to August 5, 2014.[21] According to the DAAG and AUSA, they later went to DEA headquarters and reviewed SARC files in advance of the next scheduled meeting. The OIG attended a portion of the August 5, 2014, meeting, and it was evident to us that the DAAG and AUSA had reviewed the files prior to the meeting because they began their inquiries without first reviewing the files and their questions were very specific. On August 5, 2014, after reviewing 37 long-term confidential source files in a total of more than 3 hours, the meeting was again carried over to subsequent meetings on September 3, 2014, and October 21, 2014. The OIG did not attend either of these meetings because the agreed-upon portion of the SARC meetings that the OIG was to observe concluded on August 5, 2014.

For the 2014 SARC review, the DEA's Confidential Source Unit and Office of Undercover and Sensitive Investigations prepared files with condensed versions of information contained in the DEA's official confidential source files, which are located in the field office where the source is being used. We discussed with the DAAG and AUSA the quality of documents included in the SARC files and they

---

[20] Officials from the DEA, the Criminal Division, and the OIG agreed the OIG would observe the SARC's review of 10 long-term domestic confidential sources judgmentally selected by the OIG.

[21] Because so few confidential source reviews were ultimately completed during this July 18, 2014, meeting, OIG representatives were present for the entire length of the meeting.

expressed that they were generally satisfied with the contents of the files, but that they provided suggestions to the DEA for process improvement based upon information needed to answer their questions regarding the DEA's use of the confidential source. When we examined the 2014 SARC files, we found that they were more comprehensive than the 2012 SARC files, but we also identified issues regarding the content and preparation of the files.

Our review of the files indicated to us that if the meeting had taken place as originally scheduled in 2014, the meeting participants would have received outdated information and documentation for all of the long-term confidential sources under review because the files were not updated until mid-July 2014. As noted above, the SARC meeting was originally scheduled to take place on two previous dates – June 20, 2014, and then again on July 1, 2014. The cancellation of the July 1, 2014, meeting did not occur until the late evening of the day before. However, many of the documents in the SARC files that we reviewed were dated after July 1, 2014, and immediately prior to July 18, 2014. On July 10, 2014, 1 week before the meeting ultimately occurred, DEA officials sent an e-mail request to the affected field divisions requesting more specific information related to the utilization of their long-term confidential sources, including updated justification for continued use of each of the sources up for review. DEA headquarters officials used this information in conjunction with information provided by field offices in 2013, to create and attach to each SARC file a "fact sheet." The fact sheet contained summary information on the confidential source, judicial consideration received, total payments, the source's contributions to operations, and any adverse information identified by the field office. In addition, the day before the July 18, 2014, meeting, the DEA conducted a criminal history search in the National Crime Information Center (NCIC) and a printout was included in the files. We were told that the creation of the "fact sheets" for each confidential source and inclusion of criminal history records were new tools that the DEA used to prepare for the 2014 series of meetings. Therefore, had the meeting occurred as scheduled prior to July 18, 2014, the SARC members would not have had the benefit of up-to-date status information from the field offices or updated criminal history checks.

We also found that although the DEA had recently updated a portion of the information in the SARC files, some pertinent information was outdated because it dated from the spring of 2013 when DEA headquarters first requested its field offices to provide information on the long-term sources that were being included in this SARC process. In general, the files did not include any changes to the status of the confidential sources, confidential source deactivation forms, pertinent DEA reports of investigation, or up-to-date, detailed payment information. Moreover, the SARC files did not contain information from all offices and agencies that were concurrently using the confidential source. For example, we found an instance where up to five offices concurrently used a confidential source, but information from only one of the offices was provided to the SARC. We believe that if the DEA had made more current and complete information available to the SARC, this information could have affected the consideration given and ultimately affected the SARC's approval of the continued use of the long-term confidential sources.

<u>Evaluation of the 2014 SARC Review</u>

Despite the weaknesses with the preparation and content, the 2014 SARC evaluation of long-term confidential sources appears to be drastically different than the DEA's historical patterns. This SARC review assessed the DEA's continued use of 61 long-term confidential sources over the course of a series of four documented meetings and various undocumented SARC member confidential file reviews in preparation for the meetings. The meeting minutes for these meetings totaled 68 pages and encompassed a detailed overview of what occurred during the meetings. The minutes provided specific information about each long-term confidential source, including any questions from SARC members related to the review of the confidential source's file, and formalized the DAAG's and AUSA's concurrence with the DEA's continued use of the long-term confidential source or the DEA's deactivation of the confidential source. The minutes provide the DEA with a record of each SARC file reviewed, questions and answers related to each confidential source, and instructions provided for the continued use of certain confidential sources. It is clear from these minutes that the DEA and DOJ officials conducted a more thorough review of long-term confidential source SARC files. In comparison, the meeting minutes from previous SARC meetings were between 2 and 4 pages, and provided only a vague overview of the meeting, and in 4 instances reflected that the DEA spent a total of only 15 minutes formally reviewing as a complete committee between 28 and 67 confidential source files.

The thorough review provided during the 2014 SARC meetings is appropriate for such a critical and sensitive component of the DEA's operations. Although we commend the SARC for conducting a more adequate review, we believe that the DEA should improve its preparation for and provision of information to the SARC through the development of policies specific to the process.

Untimely SARC Review

Although various DEA officials told us that they convene an annual meeting of the SARC to review the continued use of long-term confidential sources, we found that since October 2009, the SARC has only convened on two occasions. These meetings took place in February 2012 and the one meeting spanning multiple dates within 2014. We reviewed the timeliness of SARC meetings dating back to 2003, when the DEA convened its first annual SARC meeting dedicated to long-term confidential sources. As shown in the following timeline, prior to the meeting held in October 2009, the DEA convened a SARC meeting to review the use of long-term confidential sources fairly regularly every 12 to 17 months, with the longest interval being between the May 2008 and October 2009 meetings.

Figure 2

Long-term Confidential Source SARC Meeting Timeline

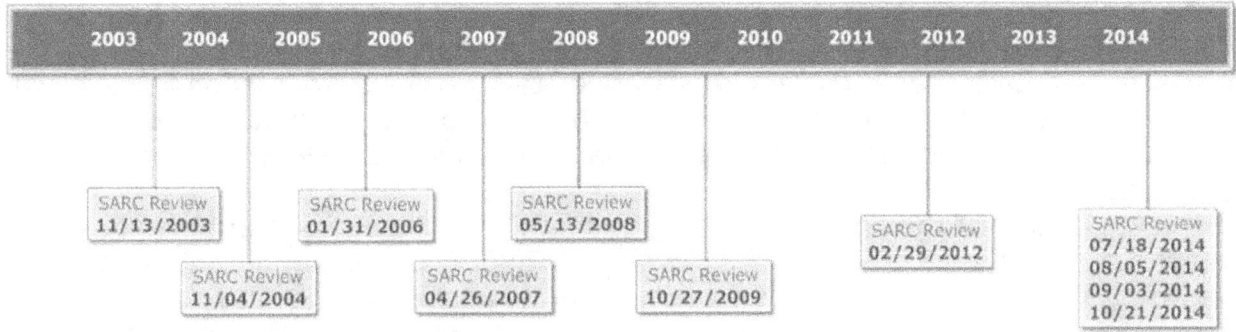

Source: OIG analysis of DEA documentation

After the October 2009 meeting, another long-term confidential source SARC meeting was not convened until February 2012, over 2 years and 4 months later. After that February 2012 meeting, the next meeting did not take place until July 2014, again more than 2 years and 4 months later. As previously noted, DEA officials explained that the reason for the delays in conducting the latest long-term SARC meeting was due to scheduling difficulties with the required officials, primarily the DAAG for the Criminal Division. DEA officials provided us with multiple e-mails dated between September 2013 and June 2014 as evidence that they had made numerous attempts to schedule a SARC meeting.

We asked the DAAG about the DEA SARC and any relevant scheduling problems and were told that there was a misunderstanding. This official informed us that, to his knowledge, the Criminal Division had not explicitly designated representatives to participate in the DEA SARC meetings for the review of long-term confidential sources.[22] The DAAG noted that he had taken part in the 2012 meeting, but he believed his participation in that long-term confidential source review was an informal invitation from the DEA because of his involvement in other DEA SARC meetings that review and approve sensitive operational activities. Therefore, when the DEA requested his participation at a long-term confidential source SARC meeting in 2013, he was unaware of his requirement to participate. Nevertheless, we believe that the DAAG could have been more responsive to the DEA's requests for assistance in scheduling a long-term confidential source SARC review.

We asked DEA officials about any additional actions that may have taken place to ensure that a timely long-term confidential SARC review occurred. We

---

[22] As previously noted, the DEA also convenes the SARC for the purpose of reviewing individual case operations of a sensitive nature. These meetings are held more frequently, but they are not calendar driven and are instead based solely on the operational needs of the DEA. According to the DAAG, DOJ has explicitly identified the DAAG as a member of these DEA "Operational SARCs." As a result, his knowledge of this formal designation and his lack of knowledge of any formal designation for long-term SARC meetings was the basis of his misunderstanding.

received varying responses and found that the DEA does not have a formal process to ensure that these SARC meetings are initiated and take place on a consistent basis. The DEA Special Agents Manual stipulates that the DEA's Confidential Source Unit and Office for Undercover and Sensitive Investigations should coordinate to ensure that a SARC reviews long-term confidential source files to determine if a confidential source should remain in an active status. However, responsible officials from these DEA entities could not describe how this coordination occurs to ensure that the SARC reviews long-term confidential sources in a timely fashion.

As a result of the DEA's recent infrequent SARC meetings, there has been a delay in the timeliness of the review and approval of DEA's continued utilization of long-term confidential sources. During the DEA's most recent SARC event that began in July 2014, the SARC reviewed sources who reached the 6-year mark immediately prior to the time when the SARC *should have met* rather than reviewing all sources who had reached that threshold as of the meeting date or another more recent cutoff date. As a result, the 2014 SARC meetings were reviewing confidential sources who were in use for 6 or more consecutive years as of the beginning of January 2013, more than 18 months prior to the start of the meeting.

Even though it was clear to us that the non-DEA members of the SARC were not familiar with the files prior to the initial session of the 2014 meeting, in the weeks prior to the SARC meeting scheduled for July 18, 2014, DEA officials from the Office of Global Enforcement and the Office of Undercover and Sensitive Investigations examined the SARC files for the long-term confidential sources being reviewed. During this review, these DEA officials identified six long-term confidential sources to deactivate before convening the first installation of the SARC meeting; two more sources were deactivated during the time period over which the meeting took place.[23] Of the eight deactivated confidential sources, one was in the United States illegally, four were no longer providing useful information or performing ongoing activities for the DEA, one had been arrested, one had been involved in an unauthorized illegal activity, and one was under investigation by the DOJ OIG. Based upon our review of the files, the information related to the DEA's reasons for deactivating some sources was available prior to the convening of the SARC. Nevertheless, the field offices responsible for overseeing these confidential sources did not deactivate them until the DEA SARC members reviewed the information and questioned the ongoing use of the confidential sources.

Although the field offices should have deactivated these confidential sources promptly, the SARC's instruction to deactivate these sources demonstrates the importance of the SARC's oversight and scrutiny of the field offices' use of long-term confidential sources. However, as a result of the significant delays in scheduling the most recent SARC, the SARC did not have the timely opportunity to ensure that the DEA's use of these confidential sources was justified. This, in

---

[23] As previously described, the July 2014 SARC meeting took place over four separate dates between July 18, 2014, and October 21, 2014.

effect, weakened the control provided for within the AG Guidelines for mitigating the risk involved in using sources over an extended period.

Absent 9-Year Interim Review

In addition to the 6-year threshold for CIRC review of confidential sources, the AG Guidelines require JLEAs to perform an internal review of long-term confidential sources 3 years after the CIRC approves the continued use of a long-term confidential source. This review is commonly referred to as the "9-year review," and is different than the 6-year threshold in that this interim review is strictly internal to the agency and no other DOJ officials are involved. We found that the DEA Special Agents Manual does not include a requirement for the DEA to conduct this type of review. However, on March 31, 2014, the DEA initiated its first-ever 9-year interim review of long-term confidential sources. According to DEA documentation, this review was initiated in an effort to bring the DEA into compliance with the AG Guidelines.

We believe that the absence of this requirement in the DEA's Special Agents Manual is significant. By not including this requirement in its policy, the DEA failed to provide proper oversight over long-term confidential sources and did not institute mitigating controls to ensure that certain risks associated with continued use of long-term confidential sources were addressed. Further, we believe that the Criminal Division's approval of the DEA's policies should be revisited to ensure that the DEA addresses the long-term source-related risks that are mitigated through the 9-year interim review requirement within the AG Guidelines.

Confidential Sources and DEA's Regulatory Function

Under federal law, all businesses that import, export, manufacture, or distribute controlled substances; all health professionals licensed to dispense, administer, or prescribe them; and all pharmacies authorized to fill prescriptions for such substances must register with the DEA. Registrants receive a DEA registration number and must comply with regulatory requirements relating to drug security and recordkeeping. The DEA uses the DEA number to facilitate the tracking of prescribed controlled substances. This regulatory function is essential to the DEA's required enforcement of the provisions of the Controlled Substances Act pertaining to the manufacturing, distribution, and dispensing of legally produced controlled substances.

Recently, we expressed concern when another DOJ law enforcement agency was found to have created a potential conflict between its investigative and regulatory functions. In the OIG's report, *A Review of ATF's Operation Fast and Furious and Related Matters*, we found that ATF, which is responsible for licensing firearms dealers, was receiving information and cooperation from an ATF licensee regarding firearms sales by the licensee to individuals who were engaged in firearms trafficking and illegal firearms purchases.[24] Our review revealed that ATF did not have controls in place to ensure that there was no conflict between its use of the individual in an investigative manner and its oversight of the same individual as an approved license holder.

Following the OIG's *Fast and Furious* review, DOJ issued guidance to its law enforcement and litigating components addressing certain risks revealed in our report. This guidance states that law enforcement protocols should include special considerations for establishing a confidential source whose business requires a license from a law enforcement agency. The guidance also states that the licensee's status as a licensee of that agency and the individual's relative compliance history should be considered in the determination of the licensee's suitability to serve as a confidential source. Such controls are important to ensure that no licensee is led to believe that the continued validity of their license is in any way predicated on their status as source.

We found that the DEA's confidential source policies do not include any specific mention of recruiting, establishing, or using sources who are also individuals with a DEA-provided controlled substance registration number. Instead, according to the DEA, it categorizes confidential sources whose business requires a license from a law enforcement agency that serves a dual-regulatory function (which would include, but is not limited to the DEA itself) as Protected Name confidential sources. Therefore, rather than implementing specific policies for these types of confidential sources, DEA processes these individuals the same as any other Protected Name confidential source. While this requires a certain level of supervisory approval, typically at the SAC level, without a stated policy that provides Special Agents with sufficient information to understand all of the implications of these relationships and the special considerations that must be taken into account, there is no assurance that DOJ's expectations will be met and there is an increased risk to DEA operations, the public, and the confidential source from the potential conflict between the source's varying relationships with the agency.

Death and Disability Payments to DEA Confidential Sources

The *Federal Employees' Compensation Act* (FECA) provides for workers' compensation coverage to federal and U.S. Postal Service workers for injuries or death sustained while in performance of duty.[25] FECA compensation can include temporary or permanent wage replacement, as well as medical and vocation benefits. The Department of Labor (DOL) is responsible for managing the FECA benefit program within the federal government and is responsible for reviewing all claims for benefits and making payments to claimants. Each employing federal agency then reimburses DOL for all FECA payments on an annual basis. According

---

[24] U.S. Department of Justice Office of the Inspector General, *A Review of ATF's Operation Fast and Furious and Related Matters*, (Re-issued November 2012).

[25] *Federal Employees' Compensation Act*, 5 U.S.C. § 8101, et seq. (2011).

to the DEA Special Agents Manual, the DEA may offer FECA benefits to confidential sources who are injured as a result of their cooperation with the DEA and to families of confidential sources killed as a result of their cooperation with the DEA.

Between July 1, 2013, and June 30, 2014, it appears that the DEA paid approximately $1,034,000 for FECA benefits to 17 confidential sources or their dependents.[26] In some cases, the DEA has been paying FECA benefits since 1974, but we could not determine the total historical cost because the DEA and DOL do not track payments to confidential sources receiving FECA benefits. In one particular case we reviewed, the confidential source was killed in July 1989 and his surviving family, which included a widow and dependents, began receiving FECA payments of $4,287 every 4 weeks. At the time of her death in 2012, the widow's 4-week payment amount had increased to $6,311. Therefore, this family alone received over $1.3 million in FECA benefits since 1989. Although the exact amount of DEA confidential source FECA payments is unknown, it is clear that significant taxpayer dollars have been expended.

We found that the DEA's administration of its confidential source FECA cases is suffering from serious mismanagement and inadequate oversight due to a lack of DEA policies and procedures for handling such cases coupled with DOL's special method for processing and administering these cases. And while the DOL FECA files show that the DEA has not submitted a confidential source FECA case since 2008, as discussed below, the DEA's policy still allows for such claims. Moreover, there are ongoing effects of the weaknesses and implications for the DEA's current policy for providing FECA benefits to confidential sources, we identify below.

Overall Weaknesses in FECA Activities Related to DEA Confidential Sources

The DEA Special Agents Manual includes two sentences stating that FECA may apply in situations where a confidential source is injured or killed as a result of their cooperation with the DEA. This policy references the DEA's Personnel Manual, which states that non-federal law enforcement officers injured or killed during the apprehension of an individual who has committed a federal crime or who is wanted in connection with a federal crime are covered by FECA and goes on to suggest that certain confidential sources may be included in this category for FECA coverage. As authority for the proposition that confidential sources may be categorized as non-federal law enforcement officers, the Personnel Manual cites Section 886 of 21 U.S.C. However, 21 U.S.C. § 886 merely discusses, among other things, the Attorney General's authority to pay confidential sources from DEA funds; it has no relationship to FECA nor does it characterize confidential sources as non-federal law enforcement officers for any purpose. Although FECA does, in some instances,

---

[26] DOL and DOJ officials could not provide us with the exact amount. The OIG calculated this estimate using a bill for the period of July 1, 2013 through June 30, 2014, provided by DOL to the DOJ's Justice Management Division (JMD), which is involved in the process of reimbursing DOL for payments related to DOJ FECA claims. In addition, although we identified 18 FECA files involving confidential sources, this estimate was calculated using information specific to 17 confidential sources because one case was declined prior to the issuance of the aforementioned bill.

extend availability for benefits to eligible law enforcement officers not employed by the United States, 5 U.S.C. § 8191, the implementing regulation defines eligible non-federal law enforcement officers only as law enforcement officers of state or local governments or governments of U.S. possessions and territories, and certain officers eligible for pensions under the D.C. Policemen and Firemen's Retirement and Disability Act.[27] Confidential sources are none of these. In our view, 21 U.S.C. § 886 does not provide a legal basis for the DEA's position that its confidential sources were appropriately categorized as non-federal law enforcement officers eligible for FECA benefits. In responding to a draft of this report, the DEA seeks to rely on 5 U.S.C. § 8101(1)(B)—which extends FECA eligibility to "an individual rendering personal service to the United States similar to the service of a civil officer or employee of the United States, without pay or for nominal pay, when a statute authorizes the acceptance or use of the service, or authorizes payment of travel or other expenses of the individual"—to characterize certain of its confidential sources as "employees" under FECA. Whatever legal authority there may be for this proposition, as noted above it is not the legal basis relied upon by the DEA in its own policies to substantiate FECA coverage, as set forth in the Personnel Manual and, by reference, the Special Agents Manual. Accordingly, we recommend that the DEA, in consultation with the Department, analyze and come to a conclusion about whether there is a legal basis and, if so, whether it is appropriate to extend eligibility for FECA benefits to confidential sources.

We also found that a number of key DEA offices lacked knowledge about its confidential source FECA activities and expenditures. For example, DEA officials with whom we spoke from the Office of Human Resources and the Office of Operations Management, in particular officials from the Confidential Source Unit, were all unaware that confidential sources were receiving FECA benefits. After numerous attempts and coordinating with entities external to the DEA, we identified two people in DEA's Office of Safety and Worker's Compensation who were aware that confidential sources were receiving FECA benefits. These DEA officials stated that the DEA does not keep any files for these FECA cases and relies solely on DOL to administer and oversee the cases. These individuals elaborated that there is almost no review of these FECA cases by any DEA headquarters officials. We were told that the field office staff forwards these cases to DEA's Office of Safety and Worker's Compensation, which reviews the forms only for clerical errors and then submits them to DOL. According to these DEA officials, after the DEA forwards the FECA case to DOL, neither the DEA field office nor headquarters is notified of DOL's acceptance or denial of the case or any other interaction between DOL and the claimant. However, DOL's Division of Federal Employees' Compensation, the division responsible for administering FECA, stated that the DEA has been notified of the acceptance or denial for every secure FECA case. DOL specified that it provides to the DEA two copies of the acceptance or denial decision – one for the DEA and the other routed through DEA for the claimant [confidential source].

---

[27] 20 C.F.R. § 10.735 (2013).

A DOL Office of Workers Compensation Programs (OWCP) official stated that DOL does not follow normal procedures for processing the DEA's confidential source FECA cases. This lead DOL official, who is currently responsible for handling these DEA cases, stated that DOL identifies these FECA cases as "secure" cases and does not perform an in-depth review of these FECA applications.[28] Further, DOL does not process any related claims through its electronic system and instead uses a labor-intensive manual process that requires a very small staff to complete the review process, maintain hard copy files, and oversee the payment transactions for all "secure" files. According to this DOL official, DOL established this structure a long time ago to accommodate the DEA's concerns regarding the sensitivity of confidential source FECA cases. We requested documentation to substantiate this statement, but neither the DOL official nor the DEA were able to provide any information to the OIG.

Inadequate Eligibility Determinations

In general, only federal employees are eligible to receive FECA benefits, but in some circumstances others may qualify for FECA benefits if the submitting agency and DOL determine that these individuals meet the criteria of a civil employee, as defined by the FECA statute and DOL regulations. We discussed confidential source eligibility with DEA and DOL officials and neither agency accepted responsibility for determining whether DEA confidential source FECA applicants met the criteria. Officials from the DEA's Office of Safety and Worker's Compensation stated that DOL is responsible for determining who is eligible for FECA benefits, while the DOL official who currently manages the DEA's confidential source FECA files stated that DOL has relied upon the DEA for the underlying determination of whether confidential sources are eligible to receive FECA benefits in accordance with the special procedure that it adopted to address DEA's concerns about the sensitivity of confidential source cases. DOL's Division of Federal Employees' Compensation clarified that DOL is the agency that determines FECA eligibility, but reiterated that, once the employing agency has identified the injured individual as a confidential source, DOL considers the definition of "employee" to have been satisfied for purposes of providing workers' compensation benefits. DOL relies on DEA and performs no independent analysis to test "employee" status.

In addition, when we discussed with the Criminal Division's Deputy Assistant Attorney General the provision of FECA benefits to DEA confidential sources, he stated that he was unaware that this was occurring. However, he indicated that if the DEA is providing FECA benefits to its confidential sources, then a prosecutor needs to know this information because it creates a financial relationship (potentially a dependent one) between the DEA and the confidential source. Based upon this DOJ official being unaware of the DEA's FECA activities related to confidential sources as well as the fact that relevant DEA officials were also

---

[28] DOL's Division of Federal Employees' Compensation acknowledged that certain aspects of case development, such as the claimant's status as a federal employee and aspects of the event leading to the injury, may not be developed or documented as they would be in a traditional claim. DOL noted, however, that other aspects of claims acceptance are followed.

generally unaware of confidential sources receiving FECA benefits, it appears that the DEA has not evaluated, or asked the Department to evaluate, how a determination that confidential sources could qualify as civil employees and receive FECA benefits might either increase the disclosure obligations of federal prosecutors in criminal cases or impact other Department equities. We believe that this is an important issue and therefore the Department should review the DEA's process for and implications of providing FECA benefits to its confidential sources.

We reviewed DOL's hard copy files for the 18 DEA confidential source FECA cases. These cases included injuries and deaths of confidential sources who were U.S. citizens and foreign nationals. During our review of these cases, we identified the event that triggered the FECA case and there were a variety of events cited. In some instances there was a clear indication that the confidential source was injured or killed while directly participating in a DEA operation. However, there were other cases for which the files were unclear on the justification for providing benefits to confidential sources or families of deceased confidential sources. In multiple cases, we could not verify or validate that DEA confidential sources were receiving FECA benefits for claims involving injuries or deaths that happened while the confidential sources were performing services directly for the DEA because the file contained insufficient information regarding the triggering event to make that determination. In fact, in one of the FECA cases that we reviewed, the FECA application included a statement from a DEA official indicating that the injury sustained by the confidential source was possibly due to the source's carelessness and that at the time of the injury the confidential source was not being directed by DEA personnel. The following are some other examples of these types of cases.

- The DEA submitted and DOL accepted a claim for a DEA confidential source who was shot and injured in 1984, but there is no indication of where and how the shooting occurred. In addition, a document in the file indicates that the confidential source "claimed" that a narcotics trafficker committed the act. We could not find any information in the file that would support that DEA officials were present when the source was injured, how they confirmed the source's claim to have been shot by a narcotics trafficker, or the basis for believing that the shooting resulted from the source's cooperation with DEA.

- The DEA submitted and DOL accepted a claim for a confidential source who was presumably killed overseas in 1991. However, according to the file, there were no witnesses to the confidential source's death and the source's body had not been recovered. The file contained no details describing how or why the DEA believed that the source was killed as a result of cooperation with the DEA.

- The DEA submitted and DOL accepted a claim for a confidential source who was shot and injured while traveling to work in 1997. This incident occurred 1 day after the DEA activated the individual as a confidential source. Further, DOL's FECA file clearly indicates that DEA officials stated that the source's injury did not happen while performing DEA-related activities. The file also indicates that the DEA had evidence that the shooting was related to the source's involvement with the DEA, but this evidence is not recounted in the DOL file nor is there an indication that the evidence was verified.

- The DOL accepted a claim that was submitted by the DEA more than 2 years after a confidential source was shot and killed at home in 1999. According to the information in the file, no DEA officials were present when the incident occurred. There was no other information in the file to indicate that the shooting occurred as a result of the confidential source's involvement with the DEA.

- The DEA submitted and DOL accepted a claim for a confidential source who was shot and injured at home in 2002. However, the file indicates that there were no witnesses to the shooting and the file contained no evidence of a link between the shooting and the individual's status as a DEA source.

Inconsistent Benefits Determination

In addition to the absence of procedures for determining eligibility of DEA confidential sources for FECA benefits, we found that there were no formal standards or policies for determining the source's "existing pay rate" at the time of the event.[29] According to DOL policy, when a recipient of FECA benefits does not receive a standard salary, DOL calculates FECA benefits using the average annual earnings for an individual who performed similar work in the previous year. Given that the services that confidential sources provide to the DEA are often irregular, sporadic, and unique in nature, the DEA's confidential sources are not paid standard amounts and there is a wide range of payments provided to confidential sources while they are active with the DEA. Therefore, in some of the FECA files we reviewed, DOL requested that the DEA provide additional information to establish the source's "existing pay rate" at the time of the injury. However, in general, we found that there was a lack of consistency in the determination of pay rates and the resulting compensation benefits determination. The following examples illustrate these inconsistencies.

- One case file indicated that a confidential source had been injured in 1994. According to the case file, the DEA provided information that the source had received approximately $10,868 in that year. DOL used that amount to establish the existing annual pay rate for the claimant. Because this amount was below DOL's established minimum compensation amount, DOL used its minimum allowable amount in establishing the recurring FECA compensation benefits for the confidential source.

- One case file indicated that a cooperating witness was killed 2 days prior to the sentencing of defendants in a DEA-related drug case in 1990. This

---

[29] An individual's existing pay rate is used to determine appropriate FECA compensation benefit amounts for injured individuals or their surviving family members. FECA compensation benefits refer to payments for lost wages due to the injury and any lasting disability. This does not refer to reimbursements for specific medical expenses.

individual had not yet received any payments from the DEA at the time of the death, but the DEA later paid the surviving family member an award payment of $10,000. To determine the existing pay rate for the deceased, DOL asked the local DEA field office to provide payment totals for its three highest paid confidential sources in the year prior to confidential source's death. The DEA provided the amounts ($174,000, $44,000, and $22,000) and recommended that the median amount be used to determine benefits. DOL agreed with the recommendation and determined the recurring FECA compensation benefit amount based upon the second highest paid DEA confidential source in the local area.

- As previously identified, the DEA filed a FECA claim for a confidential source who, 1 day after being activated as a confidential source, was shot and injured while traveling to work in 1997. Without a history of payments to this new confidential source, the DEA asked DOL to establish the source's existing pay rate by using the federal government's General Schedule (GS) pay rate for a GS-7 federal employee. DOL agreed and FECA benefits were determined based on the GS-7 pay rate.

- One case file indicated that a DEA confidential source was killed in 1991. DOL case files contain information from the DEA indicating that this source had received over $500,000 from the DEA in the prior 2 years. According to DOL, FECA benefits are capped at the maximum federal employee salary on the General Schedule, which equates to the annual pay rate for a GS-15, Step 10 employee. The file indicates that after reviewing the available information, the DOL determined that the surviving family members should receive the maximum benefit allowable, and the amount awarded at that time (1991) was $6,661 every 4 weeks.

These examples highlight the different methods used for establishing a confidential source's established annual pay rate for the determination of FECA compensation benefits for lost wages. In other files there was insufficient information related to the basis for the benefit amount. While in some cases it was clear that the responsible DEA field office was involved in the pay rate determination, there was little evidence to indicate that DEA headquarters personnel were providing any input or oversight in this area.

Active Confidential Sources Paid FECA Benefits

The purpose of FECA for injured workers is to compensate qualified individuals who are injured on the job during the time they cannot perform their duties. FECA regulations require agencies to provide assistance to injured individuals to return them to work as quickly as possible. When an employee is well enough that he or she can perform the duties that were performed prior to the injury, the individual should no longer receive FECA benefits.[30] Therefore, we believe that an active DEA source who is receiving payments from the DEA should not also be receiving regular disability compensation payments. If the DEA determines that a source who is receiving full-time disability compensation payments is suitable for active status, then the DEA should ensure that DOL is no longer providing payments to that individual. However, of the 18 confidential source FECA files, we found that the DEA continued to utilize as confidential sources at least two of the full-time disability claimants, as described below.

- For one confidential source who was injured in 1997, our review of DEA's confidential source file indicated that the DEA not only paid for this individual's housing expenses, but also provided payments for information and an award payment of over $1 million between the date of his injury and 2012. At the same time, the individual was also receiving FECA disability benefits, which amounted to approximately $2,000 every 4 weeks. The source was deactivated in 2012 because he could no longer provide useful information. He last received a source payment from DEA in October 2012. Based on DEA and DOL documentation, we estimate that between 1997 and 2012, the DEA paid this individual a total of $2,186,813, comprised of $353,075 in FECA benefits and $1,833,738 in confidential source service and award payments.

- One confidential source was receiving full FECA disability benefits resulting from an incident that occurred during a March 1986 DEA operation. However, the DEA's records indicate that the confidential source was deactivated in December 1985 and not reactivated until September 1996. DEA documentation also revealed that the DEA field office continued to pay this deactivated confidential source for information and services within months of submitting the FECA claim. One of the payments, in the amount of $1,000, was paid just 4 days after the purported injury for which the confidential source was deemed fully disabled and qualified for FECA benefits. The DEA eventually reactivated this confidential source in 1996 and as of November 2014, this individual was still an active confidential source receiving DEA payments for cooperation as well as full FECA disability benefits.

From our review of the DEA's confidential source files and DOL's FECA files it did not appear that the DEA had informed DOL of the individuals' continued use and earning as a source, or that DEA was concerned about the individuals' receiving dual benefits.

---

[30] FECA policy requires individuals receiving compensation for partial or total disability to advise OWCP immediately of any return to work, either part-time or full-time. Individuals receiving FECA benefits are also required to submit an annual report of earnings from any employment. If an individual knowingly omits or understates his or her compensation, that individual forfeits their right to benefits.

We believe that the DEA has not properly managed FECA claims for its confidential sources. Specifically, the DEA has not established a process or any controls to implement the provision of FECA benefits to confidential sources. As previously mentioned, we had great difficulty in finding anyone in the DEA with knowledge of its FECA activities related to confidential sources. Officials from the DEA Confidential Source Unit were wholly unaware of any confidential sources receiving FECA benefits and told us that it would be unlikely for the DEA to provide FECA benefits to its confidential sources. Moreover, the two individuals within the DEA's Office of Safety and Worker's Compensation with whom we spoke who were aware of the practice made it clear that they are not involved in any processing of the claims or any decision making in the cases. Further, not only does the DEA not keep any files for their own records of these FECA cases, it did not have a reliable tracking system to even identify the individual cases for which the DEA was reimbursing DOL. As a result of DEA's lack of substantive involvement and record keeping, as well as the atypical manual process DOL told us that it used for these cases at the request of DEA, we could not specifically determine how much money each recipient had been paid in FECA benefits or if the payments to the confidential sources or their families were ongoing.

In addition, neither the DEA nor DOL has accepted responsibility for judging the eligibility of FECA cases originating from confidential sources. We believe that confidential sources have been awarded FECA benefits without adequate review to verify that these individuals are legally entitled to benefits as described in the FECA statute and implementing regulations. We believe that the absence of a thorough eligibility review significantly increases the risk that taxpayer dollars will be used inappropriately.

It also appears that taxpayer dollars are at risk through the DEA's existing inconsistent process for determining an established pay rate and compensation benefits for confidential sources seeking disability payments. In some cases, FECA payment amounts were calculated based on arbitrarily selected amounts, wholly unrelated to amounts paid for any services provided by the confidential source. In other cases, pay rates were established using historical confidential source payment amounts, which may be skewed at any point in time given that the services confidential sources provide to the DEA are often irregular, sporadic, and unique in nature.

The DEA's poor oversight of its FECA activities relating to confidential sources has also resulted in the DEA inappropriately continuing to use and pay confidential sources who are receiving full disability payments through FECA and should be reporting all income to DOL. The lack of DEA policies in this area means that Special Agents in the field are left unaware of the legal and financial implications of FECA cases. In fact, one DOL case file that we reviewed contained a statement from the DEA that: "there was a lack of prescribed procedures the DEA agents are to follow in such cases, and the Special Agent had limited understanding that 'these employees' are covered under the same 'death insurance'." The DEA does not have a policy in place to facilitate informing appropriate DEA personnel about whether a confidential source is receiving FECA benefits or to verify the FECA benefits status during their normal handling of the confidential source.

As the OIG noted in its 2005 review of the DEA's Confidential Source Program, DEA officials acknowledged that confidential sources are generally not "choir boys," and the DEA must interact and rely on information from confidential sources whose credibility may be questioned. Therefore, when the DEA submits an application for a confidential source to receive FECA benefits, we believe that the DEA should employ appropriate oversight and evaluate these cases thoroughly. Although the identity of the claimants may be sensitive, this does not alleviate the DEA's responsibility to be judicious stewards of taxpayer dollars and ensure that payments are warranted. It is our opinion that the FECA-related problems we uncovered within the DEA may have broader financial and legal implications for all DOJ and other federal law enforcement agencies.

DEA officials in the Office of Workers Compensation told us in October 2014 that they have initiated a program to review DOL's FECA files related to DEA confidential sources every 6 months. However, the DEA has not indicated that it will begin keeping its own records or files related to these cases and we were not informed of any policies under development in this area.

Conclusion

The OIG initiated this audit in light of recent OIG investigations and concerns about the DEA's administration of its Confidential Source Program. Despite various instances of DEA resistance to our audit, which have impeded the OIG's ability to perform the comprehensive audit as planned, the OIG has identified certain deficiencies that we believe are indicative of inadequate oversight and management by the DEA of its Confidential Source Program.

We found deficiencies in DEA's policies in comparison to those applicable to other DOJ law enforcement components under the AG Guidelines, resulting in a failure by the DEA to mitigate a number of significant risks associated with using confidential sources. We have particular concerns about the relative lack of oversight provided to DEA confidential sources who pose the greatest risk to the U.S. government and for which the AG Guidelines specifically identify as requiring increased oversight. We believe that the DEA should promptly address these issues, and that it and the Department should re-evaluate the policies applicable to DEA confidential sources in these areas. We also are concerned that the DEA has failed to adopt policies to address the potential for conflict in the use of DEA registrants as confidential sources. And, we also believe it is extremely troubling that the DEA was almost wholly unaware of its provision of FECA benefits to confidential sources and has not effectively or judiciously managed these FECA claims.

In combination, the above mentioned deficiencies begin to demonstrate that certain aspects of the DEA's Confidential Source Program have not received the requisite level of attentiveness and require prompt improvements. Officials from the Office of the Deputy Attorney General (ODAG), Criminal Division, and DEA have confirmed that they are coordinating to improve the DEA's policies related to the management and use of confidential sources and ensuring that the policies contain all requirements included within the AG Guidelines. In addition, according to an ODAG official, the Department will initiate a review of the DEA's provision of FECA benefits to confidential sources. We intend to continue auditing the program, but encourage the DEA and the Department to continue taking corrective action and keep us informed of its efforts to improve the management of its Confidential Source Program.

Recommendations

We recommend that the DEA:

1. Coordinate with the Criminal Division to revisit the Special Agents Manual to ensure compliance with and consistent DOJ implementation of the AG Guidelines' requirements, including the following.

    a. Ensure that its confidential source policies include appropriate provisions for AG Guidelines-required special approval for the use of high-level and privileged or media-related confidential sources.

    b. Ensure that its confidential source policies include adequate information related to OIA to ensure that DEA Special Agents have an appropriate level of understanding of the risks associated with approving confidential sources in OIA.

    c. Ensure that its confidential source policies include appropriate provisions for AG Guidelines-based requirements for approving confidential sources to participate in OIA, including documenting findings, instructions, and acknowledgement of revocation of OIA authorization in the DEA's official confidential source files.

2. Ensure that its confidential source policies are updated to reflect the current practice of documenting written operations plans, including identifying the required content and approval level for those plans.

3. Develop specific policies related to the conduct of the SARC long-term confidential source review, including ensuring appropriate attendance, sufficient review procedures, and minimum file content.

4. Ensure that DEA confidential source policies are updated to ensure that long-term confidential sources are reviewed in a consistent and timely manner.

5. Ensure that its Special Agents Manual is updated to include requirements for a 9-year interim review of long-term confidential sources, in accordance with the AG Guidelines and the DEA's current practice.

6. Ensure that the DEA develops and implements appropriate policies and procedures related to establishing DEA registrants as confidential sources.

7. In consultation with the Department, analyze and come to a conclusion about whether there is a legal basis and, if so, whether it is appropriate to extend eligibility for FECA benefits to confidential sources.

   a. If the Department and DEA determine that confidential sources may be legally eligible for FECA benefits, the DEA must establish controls and policies specific to the management of existing confidential source FECA benefits and accurately memorialize the justification in DEA's policies.

   b. If the Department and DEA determine that confidential sources may be legally eligible for FECA benefits, the DEA must ensure that the confidential sources who are active with the DEA do not receive full-time FECA disability payments from DOL.

   c. If the Department and DEA determine that confidential sources may not be legally eligible for FECA benefits, the DEA must develop a process for handling the existing cases wherein benefits are being paid to confidential sources and/or their dependents.

OBJECTIVE, SCOPE, AND METHODOLOGY

Objective

The preliminary objective of our audit was to assess the DEA's management and oversight of its Confidential Source Program. Our audit work thus far has been seriously delayed by numerous instances of uncooperativeness from the DEA, including attempts to prohibit the OIG's observation of confidential source file reviews and delays, for months at a time, in providing the OIG with requested confidential source information and documentation. As a result, over 1 year after we initiated this review, the OIG only has been able to conduct a limited review of the DEA's Confidential Source Program. However, we have uncovered several significant issues related to the DEA's management of its Confidential Source Program that we believe require the prompt attention of DOJ and DEA leadership. This report provides details on our work to date, which included specifically examining the DEA's confidential source policies to ensure consistency with the AG Guidelines' requirements, reviewing the DEA's oversight of certain high-risk confidential sources and high-risk activities involving confidential sources, and evaluating the DEA's administration of death and disability benefits to confidential sources. We will continue to audit the DEA's Confidential Source Program to more fully assess the DEA's management and oversight of its confidential sources.

Scope and Methodology

We conducted this performance audit in accordance with generally accepted government auditing standards. Those standards require that we plan and perform the audit to obtain sufficient, appropriate evidence to provide a reasonable basis for our findings and conclusions based on our audit objectives. We believe that the evidence obtained provides a reasonable basis for our findings and conclusions based on our audit objectives. As previously described in this appendix, we refocused our audit work and have obtained sufficient, appropriate evidence for the findings and conclusions in this report.

To accomplish our work, we completed interviews with 31 DEA officials located in various DEA headquarters offices, including the Office of Operations Management, Office of Global Enforcement, Office of Finance, Office of Information Systems, Human Resources Division, and Inspections Division. Additionally, we spoke with 8 officials from the DEA's Chicago, San Diego, and Washington Field Divisions. We also interviewed 10 representatives from DOJ's Justice Management Division, Civil Division, and Criminal Division; as well as 1 official from the Department of Labor's Office of Workers Compensation.

We reviewed the DOJ Attorney General Guidelines Regarding the Use of Confidential Informants (AG Guidelines) and various DEA policies and procedures associated with the DEA's Confidential Source Program, including the DEA Special Agents Manual, numerous teletype and cable updates to the Special Agents Manual, and the DEA Personnel Manual. In addition, we reviewed and analyzed 65 DEA confidential source SARC files and 18 Department of Labor Federal Employees' Compensation Act (FECA) files for DEA confidential sources. We also observed a portion of the DEA's 2014 SARC meeting and analyzed documentation from the DEA's 2003 through 2012 SARC reviews of long-term confidential sources.

After reviewing the DEA's confidential source SARC files and the Department of Labor's FECA files, we judgmentally selected the Chicago and San Diego Field Divisions as locations for preliminary site visits to perform a limited review of confidential source files. During the visits, we requested and reviewed various queries from the DEA's electronic source management system and subsequently selected and reviewed 17 confidential source files for more detailed analysis. We also reviewed three closed investigative case files that were referred to in two of the confidential source files.

We did not as, part of this review, evaluate the DEA's overall compliance with all laws and regulations or evaluate all of the DEA's internal controls over its Confidential Source Program. However, this report does provide some finding areas that indicate a risk of non-compliance and weak internal controls. As stated in the report, the OIG will continue auditing the DEA's Confidential Source Program to ensure that we fully address our original audit objective to assess the DEA's management and oversight of its confidential sources.

CROSSWALK BETWEEN THE DEA AND AG GUIDELINES CONFIDENTIAL SOURCE CATEGORIES

OIG REQUEST FOR INFORMATION PERTAINING TO THE CONFIDENTIAL SOURCE PROGRAM

September 12, 2014

QUESTION #12: Provide an overview of how all DEA CS categories identified in the Agents Manual correspond to the different types of CS categories mentioned within the Attorney General Guidelines.

AG Guidelines: Confidential Informant or CI – any individual who provides useful and credible information to a JLEA regarding felonious criminal activities, and from whom the JLEA expects or intends to obtain additional useful and credible information regarding such activities in the future.

DEA categories corresponding to the guidelines above:

> **Regular Use** - does not meet the guidelines established for Restricted, Defendant or Protected Name use.

> **Restricted Use** – An individual who will be subject to a greater degree of supervisory control than a Regular Use CS based upon factors within his/her background that indicates a need for such supervision.

> **Protected Name** – An individual whose public identification or utilization as a DEA CS could pose a threat to the national security of the U.S. or a foreign country, or result in a high likelihood of violence to the CS and/or his/her family members or associates, or is likely to raise complex legal issues.

AG Guidelines: Cooperating Defendant/Witness - any individual who:

Meets the definition of a CI; has agreed to testify in a proceeding as a result of having provided information to the JLEA; and is a defendant or potential witness who has a written agreement with a FPO, pursuant to which the individual has an expectation of future judicial or prosecutive consideration or assistance as a result of having provided information to the JLEA, or is a potential witness who has had a FPO concur in all material aspects of his or her use by the JLEA.

DEA category corresponding to the guidelines above:

> **Defendant Confidential Source** – A Defendant CS has been arrested or is subject to arrest and prosecution for a federal or state offense. This individual may or may not expect future consideration for his/her cooperation in the form of judicial or prosecution consideration or assistance.

AG Guidelines: Source of Information – any individual who:

Meets the definition of a CI; provides information to a JLEA solely as a result of legitimate routine access to information or records, such as an employee of the military, a law enforcement agency, or a legitimate business (e.g., phone company, banks, airlines), and not as a result of criminal association with persons of investigative interest to the JLEA; and provides such information in a manner consistent with applicable law.

DEA categories corresponding to the guidelines above:

> **Limited Use** – A CS established for payment purposes only and is a professional business person or a tipster. This person may be recruited by DEA but must provide information independently (without directions by DEA); This person would not be required to testify as a witness in any legal proceeding, DEA could corroborate the information supplied by the CS independently; DEA anticipates rewarding this person for information/services rendered; the information obtained by this person is not provided as a result of criminal association with persons of investigative interest to DEA.

> **Protected Name** – An individual whose public identification or utilization as a DEA CS could pose a threat to the national security of the U.S. or a foreign country, or result in a high likelihood of violence to the CS and/or his/her family members or associates, or is likely to raise complex legal issues.

AG Guidelines: High Level Confidential Informant: - a CI who is part of the senior leadership of an enterprise that has a national or international sphere of activities, or high significance to the JLEA's national objectives, even if the enterprise's sphere of activities is local or regional; and engages in, or uses others to commit, any of the conduct described below in paragraph (I) (B) (10) (b) (i)-(iv).

DEA categories corresponding to the guidelines above: This solely depends on what happens during the investigation.

> **Regular Use** - does not meet the guidelines established for Restricted, Defendant or Protected Name use.

> **Restricted Use** – An individual who will be subject to a greater degree of supervisory control than a Regular Use CS based upon factors within his/her background that indicates a need for such supervision.

> **Protected Name** – An individual whose public identification or utilization as a DEA CS could pose a threat to the national security of the U.S. or a foreign country, or result in a high likelihood of violence to the CS and/or his/her family members or associates, or is likely to raise complex legal issues.

Defendant Confidential Source – A Defendant CS has been arrested or is subject to arrest and prosecution for a federal or state offense. This individual may or may not expect future consideration for his/her cooperation in the form of judicial or prosecution consideration or assistance.

THE DEPARTMENT OF JUSTICE'S
RESPONSE TO THE DRAFT AUDIT REPORT

U. S. Department of Justice

Office of the Deputy Attorney General

Associate Deputy Attorney General   *Washington, D.C. 20530*

June 30, 2015

MEMORANDUM

TO: Carol S. Taraszka
           Regional Audit Manager
           Office of the Inspector General

FROM: Daniel Grooms
           Associate Deputy Attorney General
           Office of the Deputy Attorney General

SUBJECT: Department's Response to Draft Report of the Office of the Inspector General:
           Audit of the Drug Enforcement Administration's Confidential Source Program

We appreciate the review undertaken by the Department of Justice (Department) Office of the Inspector General (OIG) entitled *Audit of the Drug Enforcement Administration's Confidential Source Program.* The OIG report contains seven recommendations; the Department concurs in all seven. Although the Audit is focused exclusively on DEA's Confidential Source (CS) Program, and accordingly the responses to the recommendations below are addressed from the perspective of DEA, because the report addresses issues that go beyond DEA and require the participation of multiple Departmental components, this response is being submitted by the Office of the Deputy Attorney General.

Recognizing that the use of confidential informants in criminal investigations and prosecutions presents unique risks both to the safety of agents, informants, targets, and others, and to the viability and integrity of the investigations and prosecutions in which the informants participate, in 2002, the Attorney General issued Guidelines Regarding the Use of Confidential Informants (AG Guidelines). These Guidelines were created both to establish policies for the use of confidential informants in criminal investigations and prosecutions and to establish the criteria for procedures that are necessary to the implementation of those policies. The Department remains committed to ensuring that its law enforcement agencies maintain and consistently implement policies and procedures regarding the use of confidential informants that comply with both the AG Guidelines and the Department's overall approach to risk assessment and mitigation.

In addition to the recommendations addressed below, in its report OIG raises concerns about DEA's lack of cooperation with the audit team. While we believe that DEA's goal throughout this process has been to cooperate with the OIG review consistent with their obligations to protect the agency's CS Program, we regret any delays to OIG's work. The

Department and DEA remain committed to working with OIG to ensure OIG receives all of the information necessary to complete its reviews and understand that DEA and OIG have now resolved all concerns regarding access to information and materials.

The Department appreciates the opportunity to respond to the OIG's audit and is committed to working with the OIG as it continues its review of DEA's CS Program.

Recommendation 1: Coordinate with the Criminal Division to revisit the Special Agents Manual to ensure compliance with and consistent DOJ implementation of the AG Guidelines' requirements.

    a. **Ensure that its confidential source policies include appropriate provision for AG Guidelines – required special approval for the use of high – level and privileged or media-related confidential sources.**

    b. **Ensure that its confidential source policies include adequate information related to OIA to ensure that DEA Special Agents have an appropriate level of understanding of the risks associated with approving confidential sources in OIA.**

    c. **Ensure that its confidential source policies include appropriate provisions for AG Guidelines-based requirements for approving confidential sources to participate in OIA, including documenting findings, instructions, and acknowledgement of revocation of OIA authorization in the DEA's official confidential source files.**

DEA concurs in this recommendation. Consistent with the roles and responsibilities established by the AG Guidelines, in December 2014, the Deputy Attorney General directed DEA and the Criminal Division to conduct a comprehensive process to review and revise the DEA Agents' Manual to ensure that DEA's policies comply with the AG Guidelines and are presented in a manner that is consistent with the AG Guidelines in both form and function. That review is ongoing, and when completed, the revised policies will include provisions governing the registration of high-level, privileged, and media-related confidential sources. The revised policies will also clarify the requirements necessary to approve Otherwise Illegal Activity (OIA) and will require agents to document the information necessary to apply the principles of risk assessment and mitigation when authorizing and executing OIA.

Recommendation 2: Ensure that its confidential source policies are updated to reflect the current practice of documenting written operations plans, including identifying the required content and approval level for those plans.

DEA concurs in this recommendation. The ongoing review and revision of the Agents' Manual, which DEA is conducting in consultation with the Criminal Division, will clarify the required content for written operations plans and other forms the DEA uses to document the authorization of OIA, instructions given to confidential sources, and the confidential sources' acknowledgment of the same. The revisions to the Agents' Manual also will address how such forms will be maintained consistent with the AG Guidelines.

Recommendation 3: Develop specific policies related to the conduct of the SARC long-term confidential source review, including ensuring appropriate attendance, sufficient review

procedures, and minimum file content.

DEA concurs in this recommendation. The ongoing review and revision of the Agents' Manual, which DEA is conducting in consultation with the Criminal Division, will ensure that the review of long-term confidential sources satisfies the AG Guidelines both in the written policies and their implementation.

Recommendation 4: Ensure that DEA confidential source policies are updated to ensure that long-term confidential sources are reviewed in a consistent and timely manner.

DEA concurs in this recommendation. As with Recommendation 3 above, the ongoing review and revision of the Agents' Manual, which DEA is conducting in consultation with the Criminal Division, will ensure that the review of long-term confidential sources satisfies the AG Guidelines both in the written policies and their implementation.

Recommendation 5: Ensure that its Special Agents Manual is updated to include requirements for a 9-year interim review of long-term confidential sources, in accordance with the AG Guidelines and the DEA's current practice.

DEA concurs in this recommendation. As with Recommendations 3 and 4 above, the ongoing review and revision of the Agents' Manual, which DEA is conducting in consultation with the Criminal Division, will ensure that the review of long-term confidential sources satisfies the AG Guidelines both in the written policies and their implementation.

Recommendation 6: Ensure that the DEA develops and implements appropriate policies and procedures related to establishing DEA registrants as confidential sources.

DEA concurs in this recommendation. The ongoing review process discussed above will ensure that the Agents' Manual addresses the use of registrants as confidential sources and includes policies governing such use.

Recommendation 7: In consultation with the Department, analyze and come to a conclusion about whether there is a legal basis and, if so, whether it is appropriate to extend eligibility for FECA benefits to confidential sources.

a. **If the Department and DEA determine that confidential sources may be legally eligible for FECA benefits, the DEA must establish controls and policies specific to the management of existing confidential source FECA benefits and accurately memorialize the justification in DEA's policies.**
b. **If the Department and DEA determine that confidential sources may be legally eligible for FECA benefits, the DEA must ensure that the confidential sources who are active with the DEA do not receive full-time FECA disability payments from DOL.**
c. **If the Department and DEA determine that confidential sources may not be legally eligible for FECA benefits, the DEA must develop a process for handling the existing cases wherein benefits are being paid to confidential sources and/or their**

dependents.

DEA concurs in this recommendation. As an initial matter, pending resolution of this issue, DEA placed a moratorium on the transmission of new FECA claims for confidential sources to the Department of Labor. DEA also has revisited the question whether confidential sources may qualify for FECA benefits and has determined that, while the ultimate determination must be made based on the facts and circumstances of each individual case, as a presumptive matter, confidential sources are not "employees" pursuant to FECA and therefore are not eligible for FECA benefits because confidential sources do not perform services "similar to the service of a civil officer or employee of the United States." In the extraordinary circumstance where a confidential source met the statutory criteria to qualify as an employee, DEA concurs with the recommendation that it must establish controls and policies for the provision and supervision of any benefits to which an individual is entitled. DEA further concurs that it must establish controls and policies for existing individuals receiving FECA benefits to the extent such benefits continue to be provided. Accordingly, the Human Resource (HR) Division, Office of the Deputy Assistant Administrator for HR, will develop a process with the Department of Labor (DOL) to manage any benefits requests and will develop internal operating procedures to ensure proper claim review/justification, tracking, monitoring, recordkeeping, secure storage, and notification to appropriate DEA office(s). DEA's Confidential Source Unit also will coordinate with the DEA's Office of Chief Counsel and HR to establish policies and controls regarding the FECA benefits process. The new policy and controls will address any potential future recipients, should there be any, and provide guidance in addressing the handling of current recipients. Included within these policies will be mechanisms to prevent active confidential sources for DEA or other law enforcement agencies from receiving FECA disability payments.

OFFICE OF THE INSPECTOR GENERAL
ANALYSIS AND SUMMARY OF ACTIONS
NECESSARY TO CLOSE THE REPORT

The Office of the Inspector General (OIG) provided a draft of this audit report to the Drug Enforcement Administration (DEA), the Office of the Deputy Attorney General (ODAG), and the Criminal Division. As noted in the consolidated response submitted by the ODAG, although this audit focused exclusively on DEA's Confidential Source Program, the report addresses issues that require the participation of multiple DOJ components. As such, the responses provided are addressed from the DEA's perspective, but include the Department's acknowledgement of its commitment to ensuring DOJ law enforcement agencies maintain and consistently implement policies and procedures regarding the use of confidential informants that comply with both the AG Guidelines and the Department's overall approach to risk assessment and mitigation. This consolidated response is incorporated in Appendix 3 of this final report. The following provides the OIG analysis of the response and summary of actions necessary to close the report.

Recommendations:

1. **Coordinate with the Criminal Division to revisit the Special Agents Manual to ensure compliance with and consistent DOJ implementation of the AG Guidelines' requirements, including the following.**

   a. **Ensure that its confidential source policies include appropriate provisions for AG Guidelines-required special approval for the use of high-level and privileged or media-related confidential sources.**

   b. **Ensure that its confidential source policies include adequate information related to OIA to ensure that DEA Special Agents have an appropriate level of understanding of the risks associated with approving confidential sources in OIA.**

   c. **Ensure that its confidential source policies include appropriate provisions for AG Guidelines-based requirements for approving confidential sources to participate in OIA, including documenting findings, instructions, and acknowledgement of revocation of OIA authorization in the DEA's official confidential source files.**

   Resolved. The DEA concurred with our recommendation. In its response on DEA's behalf, the ODAG stated that, at the direction of the Deputy Attorney General, the DEA and the Criminal Division are currently conducting a comprehensive review of the Special Agents Manual to ensure that the DEA's policies comply with the AG Guidelines and are presented in a manner consistent with the AG Guidelines in both form and function. The response further stated the revised policies will include provisions governing the registration of high-level, privileged, and media-related confidential sources. Additionally, it indicated that the revised policies will require agents to document the information necessary to approve Otherwise Illegal Activity (OIA) and will require agents to document the information necessary to apply principles of risk assessment and mitigation when authorizing and executing OIA.

This recommendation can be closed when we receive evidence that the DEA, in coordination with the Criminal Division, has established and implemented new AG Guidelines-compliant policies for the use of confidential sources who meet the requirements for special approval. In addition, please provide evidence that the policies include specific AG Guidelines requirements for authorizing, instructing, and revoking a confidential source's participation in OIA and documenting this information in the confidential source file.

2. **Ensure that its confidential source policies are updated to reflect the current practice of documenting written operations plans, including identifying the required content and approval level for those plans.**

    Resolved. The DEA concurred with our recommendation. In its response on DEA's behalf, the ODAG stated that the ongoing review and revision of the Special Agents Manual will clarify the required content for written operations plans and other forms the DEA uses to document the authorization of OIA, instructions given to confidential sources, and the confidential sources' acknowledgement of the same. The response further stated that the revisions will also address how such forms will be maintained consistent with the AG Guidelines. However, the response did not identify the inclusion of required approval levels for operations plans in the revised policies.

    This recommendation can be closed when we receive evidence that the DEA has established and implemented new policies that reflect the DEA's current practice of documenting written operations plans, including the required approval levels for operations.

3. **Develop specific policies related to the conduct of the SARC long-term confidential source review, including ensuring appropriate attendance, sufficient review procedures, and minimum file content.**

    Resolved. The DEA concurred with our recommendation. In its response on DEA's behalf, the ODAG stated that the ongoing review and revision of the Special Agents Manual will ensure that the review of long-term confidential sources satisfies the AG Guidelines both in the written policies and their implementation.

    This recommendation can be closed when we receive evidence that the DEA has established and implemented new policies that comply with all

AG Guidelines requirements for the SARC review of long-term confidential sources.

4. **Ensure that DEA confidential source policies are updated to ensure that long-term confidential sources are reviewed in a consistent and timely manner.**

    Resolved. The DEA concurred with our recommendation. In its response on DEA's behalf, the ODAG stated that the ongoing review and revision of the Special Agents Manual will ensure that the review of long-term confidential sources satisfies the AG Guidelines both in the written policies and their implementation. We believe that ensuring the manual satisfies the AG Guidelines is the correct approach, but also believe that these revisions should include sufficient detail regarding the procedures for executing the long-term SARC review of confidential sources to ensure the continuity of those processes.

    This recommendation can be closed when we receive evidence that the DEA has established and implemented new policies and procedures that comply with all AG Guidelines requirements for the SARC review of long-term confidential sources, including sufficient detail to ensure the continuity of those processes.

5. **Ensure that its Special Agents Manual is updated to include requirements for a 9-year interim review of long-term confidential sources, in accordance with the AG Guidelines and the DEA's current practice.**

    Resolved. The DEA concurred with our recommendation. In its response on DEA's behalf, the ODAG stated that the ongoing review and revision of the Special Agents Manual will ensure that the review of long-term confidential sources satisfies the AG Guidelines both in the written policies and their implementation.

    This recommendation can be closed when we receive evidence that the DEA has established and implemented new policies that comply with the AG Guidelines requirements for a 9-year interim review of long-term confidential sources, including sufficient detail to ensure process continuity.

6. **Ensure that the DEA develops and implements appropriate policies and procedures related to establishing DEA registrants as confidential sources.**

    Resolved. The DEA concurred with our recommendation. In its response on DEA's behalf, the ODAG stated that the ongoing review and revision of the Special Agents Manual will address the use of registrants as confidential sources and will include policies governing such use.

This recommendation can be closed when we receive evidence that the DEA has established and implemented appropriate policies and procedures related to the establishment and use of DEA registrants as confidential sources.

7. **In consultation with the Department, analyze and come to a conclusion about whether there is a legal basis and, if so, whether it is appropriate to extend eligibility for FECA benefits to confidential sources.**

   a. **If the Department and DEA determine that confidential sources may be legally eligible for FECA benefits, the DEA must establish controls and policies specific to the management of existing confidential source FECA benefits and accurately memorialize the justification in DEA's policies.**

   b. **If the Department and DEA determine that confidential sources may be legally eligible for FECA benefits, the DEA must ensure that the confidential sources who are active with the DEA do not receive full-time FECA disability payments from DOL.**

   c. **If the Department and DEA determine that confidential sources may not be legally eligible for FECA benefits, the DEA must develop a process for handling the existing cases wherein benefits are being paid to confidential sources and/or their dependents.**

Resolved. The DEA concurred with our recommendation. In its response on DEA's behalf, the ODAG stated that the DEA placed a moratorium on the transmission of new FECA claims for confidential sources to the Department of Labor, pending resolution of this issue. The response further stated that the DEA has determined that, as a presumptive matter, confidential sources are not 'employees' pursuant to FECA and are therefore not eligible for FECA benefits because confidential sources do not perform services "similar to the service of a civil officer or employee of the United States." However, the response acknowledged that the ultimate determination of FECA eligibility must be made based on the facts and circumstances of each individual case. As such, for the extraordinary circumstances where a confidential source met the statutory criteria to qualify as an employee, the DEA stated that it will establish internal operating procedures, policies, and controls for the FECA benefits process and will coordinate with the Department of Labor to develop a process to manage benefits requests. According to the response, these policies and procedures will include mechanisms that will prevent active confidential sources for DEA or other law enforcement agencies from receiving FECA disability payments. Moreover, the response indicated that these policies, controls, and procedures will address any potential future recipients, should there be any, and provide guidance in addressing the handling of current recipients.

This recommendation can be closed when we receive evidence that the DEA, in consultation with the ODAG and the Criminal Division, has established and implemented new policies that include provisions related to oversight and management of confidential source FECA claims and benefits, as necessary to act in accordance with the Department's presumptive and a future final decision regarding the appropriateness of extending FECA benefits to confidential sources. In addition, this recommendation can be closed when we receive evidence that the DEA, in coordination with the Department, has reviewed and agreed on the continuance or cessation of the provision of the current ongoing FECA benefits to confidential sources.